WHAT IT TAKES
TO SAVE A LIFE

WHAT IT TAKES TO SAVE A LIFE

A Veterinarian's Quest for Healing
and Hope

Dr. Kwane Stewart

HARPERONE
An Imprint of HarperCollins*Publishers*

WHAT IT TAKES TO SAVE A LIFE. Copyright © 2023 by Dr. Kwane Stewart.
All rights reserved. No part of this book may be used or reproduced in any
manner whatsoever without written permission except in the case of brief
quotations embodied in critical articles and reviews. For information,
address HarperCollins Publishers,
195 Broadway, New York, NY 10007.

HarperCollins books may be purchased for educational, business, or
sales promotional use. For information, please email the Special Markets
Department at SPsales@harpercollins.com.

FIRST PAPERBACK EDITION PUBLISHED BY HARPERCOLLINS IN 2025

Library of Congress Cataloging-in-Publication Data is
available upon request.

ISBN 978-0-06-321583-2

$PrintCode

This is dedicated to the many wonderful people I have met in the streets during my twelve-year journey. Your perseverance and dedication to your companions is unmatched.

No one will ever touch you so lightly they won't leave a trace.

—Anonymous

AUTHOR'S NOTE

I have tried my utmost in writing this book to be true to the experiences of my life and the lives of those I've met. That said, in the interest of protecting the privacy of the people I've encountered through the years, I've changed some names and identifying details. I have also, on occasion, compacted timelines.

INTRODUCTION

The sun was bright overhead as my fiancée, Amber, and I walked along Mission Beach. But then again, the sun was almost always bright—this *was* San Diego. We lived up in the hills and hadn't yet been to Mission Beach together. We wanted to do something special to mark our engagement, just the two of us, and a walk along the beach and lunch out felt celebratory.

Behind us, kids screamed from the roller coaster at the beach's amusement park. On the sand in front of us, surfers got their boards ready. Bodybuilders cruised around the boardwalk to see how much attention they could attract. Tourists and locals alike set up beach chairs and took selfies. Homeless teens, men, and women hung out closer to the boardwalk than the surf, but not in groups. I knew they didn't want to attract the notice of authorities who might kick them out. They hadn't set up tents or anything—that wasn't allowed on Mission Beach. But some held signs asking for money, most had their belongings all bundled beside them, and they looked at once aimless and completely at home.

As we passed a concrete wall along one section of the boardwalk,

Amber said something about the place where we were going to have lunch, but I wasn't really listening. I'd been overcome by a strong wave of déjà vu. I remembered everything about that spot—the smells of fried fish and sweet ice cream, the amusement park screams and the sound of the surf, the sun beating down. Amber had no idea, but we'd just passed the spot where, nearly twenty-five years before, I had sat against that wall, staring at the ocean waves, and seriously contemplated taking my life.

I'd been in my late twenties at the time, a new veterinarian seemingly living my dream: residing in sunny San Diego; getting to work with animals all day at my dream job; finally, *finally* out of school. But something had gone very wrong since my first week of vet school, when I'd felt baffled to learn about a graduating senior who'd killed himself—why would someone do that when they were so close to such a massive achievement? The day I sat against that wall, I thought I knew. I thought that graduating senior might just have been on to something.

I've often wondered about the particular makeup of those who go into veterinary medicine. We tend to be highly sensitive, which is probably what attracted us to working with animals in the first place. And yet the field itself is grueling and often heartbreaking. Sensitive people aren't wired for tasks like putting an animal to sleep because its owner can't afford to pay for the treatment it needs. Sensitive people aren't wired to treat animals that have been severely neglected. Sensitive people aren't always cut out for the hard-edged business side of the industry: the student debt, the workplace churn, the necessity of putting a beloved pet to sleep and comforting the owner one minute, then the next minute greeting another owner with a new puppy, as if nothing has just happened. And yet those are tasks we have to do all the time.

It wasn't just the strains of the job that led me to contemplate suicide that day, though. It was a confluence of stressors—professional, yes, but also financial, medical, and emotional. But as I'd stared at the ocean, I knew I had one of two choices: I could slam a bunch of pills I had in my pocket and walk myself into the waves, or I could walk myself to a hospital. I chose the hospital.

Eighteen years later, I'd had another memorable encounter in almost exactly the same spot. I'd been in my forties, and Mission Beach had become one of my regular spots to do my "street work," my informal practice of treating animals of the homeless. I was walking around with Genesis, the vet tech who assisted me, when we met Don and his blind dachshund, Loca. Don had had a rough go from the moment he'd been diagnosed with cancer. Medical expenses and some financial mistakes caused him to lose his home, and he and Loca had been on the streets ever since. He was still pretty sick when I encountered him that day. He had lost not just his home, but his boat and his livelihood. He didn't talk about family, and I'm not sure he had any friends. But he wasn't staring out at the waves wondering whether to end it all. He never would, because Loca needed him. Everything he did, every decision he made, was for that dog. She was his world, and he was hers.

I've heard similar stories in the years I've been involved in helping the homeless—stories of people who have lost everything but their animal, people who have been ignored, derided, and who have made their share of mistakes, whether they be financial, chemical, or interpersonal. Again and again I've heard of people living for the sake of their animal, how their animal has helped them heal. But there was something about Don and his blind pup that stayed with me more than all the others. Something memorable about the steely look in Don's eye that said, *It's hard, but we're survivors.*

Loca saved Don. And helping animals like Loca, and people like Don, would end up saving me.

Chapter 1

ENDLESS ROWS OF CAGES

I just had time to close my office door before the room started spinning. I'd become familiar with what panic attacks felt like, and I had sensed one coming on moments ago while I was in the lobby surrounded by my staff. Thankfully, I made it to my office before any of them had seen. *Sit. Breathe.* I felt for my desk chair, slumped down, and put my head in my hands. *It's okay. You're okay.* I looked down at the scuffed linoleum floor, trying to get my eyes to focus on its many cracks and stains. The door did little to muffle the din of the shelter. The dogs barking and crying. The cats howling. The brisk, commanding voice of my right-hand vet tech, Paisley, barking orders to the other techs. *Breathe. Focus. Calm.*

It wasn't my first panic attack at the shelter. Nor was it surprising, as it had been *a day*, and it was only 10 a.m. Mornings were always the worst. Some people start their workday with coffee and company-wide meetings. I started my workday by touring the kennels and deciding which animals had to be euthanized. So many animals. I had more than four hundred in my care at any given time. Each morning I'd go on my rounds, Paisley beside me with a clipboard, and assess where we were. How many animals had come in, how many could we save? That morning, my rounds had been brutal. I'd had to put seventy animals—many of them healthy—on the "PTS," or "put to sleep" list.

I knew what the public around our clinic thought of us. The Stanislaus County Animal Shelter was thirty-five years old but could have been one hundred. It looked like an old, creepy sanitarium, smelled like sewage, and had one of the highest euthanasia rates in the entire country. The paint was worn and the concrete cracked. There were few windows, and it was enclosed in old barbed-wire fence, like a prison. We were a death house, and I was the death dealer in chief. Animal lovers made villains of us and gave their donations to "no kill" shelters. What they didn't know is that those shelters had options we didn't have. They could take in the animals they knew for certain they could adopt out. They'd never take the three-legged pit bull that had been dropped on our doorstep, because they didn't have to. They didn't have to take the litters and litters of kittens that needed to be bottle-fed. They didn't have to take the mutt who'd been hit by a car in the middle of the night and picked up by animal control, or the elderly cat infested with fleas. The Stanislaus County Animal Shelter was the last stop, the last hope for animals that had nowhere else to go. We saved some of them—there were great victories, homes found and animals given second chances. But we saved far fewer than I wanted to.

Euthanizing animals had not been part of my vision when I decided to become a veterinarian. I wanted to save them, to heal them. One of my strongest childhood memories was of seeing an injured dog on the drive to school when I was seven. It was more than forty years ago, but I can still see that dog in my mind. With the expertise I now have, I can say it was a golden retriever, maybe a year and a half old, and about fifty-five pounds, likely female. The dog was running from yard to yard, and I could see that there was something wrong with her ear—it looked like half of it had been torn off, and it was bleeding.

"Stop the car!" I yelled to my mom from the backseat. "That dog's hurt."

"It's okay, Kwane," my mom said. "You're going to be late for school. I'm sure the dog is just going home."

"But Mom—"

"I'll look for her after I drop you off, okay?" she said. My mom was a huge animal lover, so I was somewhat reassured.

When she picked me up that afternoon, I didn't say hello before I asked if she'd found the dog.

"No," she said. "I'm sorry, honey."

All that evening, I worried about the dog. She was hurt—what if she didn't find her family before it got dark? What if she was in pain? What if she was scared? I remember going to bed that night with an unsettled feeling. How could I be safe and warm in my bedroom when she was out there, lost? We had to find that dog. We had to find that dog and help her.

The next day on the way to and from school, I kept my eyes peeled for the flash of golden fur but didn't see anything. I couldn't imagine another night of not knowing if she was okay, so I went back to where I'd last seen her to look for her on my own. And sure enough, after wandering the neighborhood for what felt like hours I saw her, again running through different yards along the side of the street.

"Here, pup!" I called, but the dog ran from me. I chased her through several yards, and finally got within about twenty feet of her. I could see her ear better now. It had turned black and crusty.

"C'mon, pup," I said in a voice that I hoped sounded calm and reassuring. "Come here, pup." She stopped running but wouldn't let me get any closer. I crouched down and extended a hand, hoping she'd come for it. She stared at me, measuring me up with her questioning, deep brown eyes. I tried to look as harmless as possible, but she wouldn't come any closer. Why hadn't I thought to bring any snacks?

I don't know if I flinched, or shifted my weight too quickly, but something I did set her off running again. She was out of my sight within seconds.

I went home defeated. My mom tried to make me feel better, and promised me she'd drive the streets with me the next day after school to look for the dog. She kept her promise, and we searched and searched the next day, but no dog. My mom sighed and told me what I can now see was a white lie. "Kwane," she said, her voice kind, "I'm sure she has an owner—they've found her by now. That's why we haven't seen her."

I believed her enough to let it go, or at least not to hold on as tightly. I didn't beg her to drive the streets around school every day anymore. And after a few weeks, I didn't look for flashes of golden fur. But my mind kept going over the afternoon I'd gotten so close to her. Could I have done something differently? Would she have come to me if I had? What if I'd had treats with me? What if I hadn't flinched? Could I have saved her? I vowed that I'd never have an encounter like that again, where I felt so powerless. If I saw a dog that was hurting, I'd do anything I could to help it.

Not long afterward, my mom took me to see *The Black Stallion*, and I was transfixed. It did for me what *Star Wars* had done for so many of my friends, but instead of obsessing over the *Millennium Falcon* racing through space, I was made speechless by images of a black horse racing through the night. As soon as the lights came up at the end of that movie, I announced to my mom that I was going to be a veterinarian.

From that day forward, I never wavered. I was a track star of sorts in high school, and given that my dad had played for the NFL, and given that I am six-three and an athletically built Black man, others looked at me and categorized me as "athlete." Once a track coach from another team asked me, "So what do you wanna do when you get older?" And I said, "I'm going to be a veterinarian." He chuckled and said, "I've never met a Black veterinarian before."

"Well, then I'm going to be the first one you know," I shot back. Notably, this coach was Black himself.

"I just think you're a great athlete," he continued. "Don't give that up."

It was the typical "Blacks do sports" trope. Looking back, I actually feel sorry for the guy. He couldn't fathom a young Black kid growing up and becoming a veterinarian. He himself would never have been offered the chance.

I took his doubt as a challenge. All throughout college at the

University of New Mexico, when career advisers and curious professors asked my intentions, it was always the same. I was going to be a vet, and I was going to heal animals. I was accepted into Colorado State's veterinary school, where sure enough, I was one of only two Black students in the entire school.

I was ready. On the first day of orientation, I picked up my welcome packet and badge, and took the dean's invitation to all of us first years to walk around the facilities and become familiar with our new home. I wandered into the anatomy lab, a cafeteria-sized room with rows of stainless-steel surgical tables. The room had a cold feel with a strong formaldehyde odor. In the far corner I saw a walk-in refrigeration unit, the door cracked as a dispassionate worker in rubber boots sprayed the floor. Behind him I caught a glimpse of large hanging carcasses: a horse, a cow, a sheep, maybe a llama.

Various organs sat in jars around the outer edge of the room. I came to a skull, just small enough to rest in the palm of my hand, perched on a shelf. I was certain it was the head of a cat, and turned it this way and that, taking it all in. Another wandering student headed in my direction. "Do you know what this is?" I asked, holding up the skull. She casually pointed her index finger to the wall where a marker read: SKULL OF 5 YEAR OLD GREYHOUND. I set it back on the shelf, embarrassed. "Wow," I murmured to myself. "I don't know a damn thing." I was terrified and absolutely elated. This was where I was meant to be, and this day marked the beginning of what I was destined to do.

And now here I was, more than a decade later and well into my career as a veterinarian, mired in a den of barking dogs and endless rows of cages. Charles Darwin once wrote, "Love for all living creatures is the most noble attribute of man," but I was so far re-moved from that vet student I'd once been that I wasn't sure what love had to do with any of it.

The office around me had come back into focus, and my breathing had steadied. But I felt shaky, not at all ready to go back out to the main shelter and be the leader my staff needed me to be. Though I was in a dark place that morning, the banter among the all-female staff outside my office door was going strong. They went about their work and I could hear one say, "Where did Doc Stewy go?" They'd adopted the nickname for me for god-knows-why. But I accepted it with reasonably good humor, the same way I accepted their teasing me about my love life. The fact of the matter was, they knew when it was time to be serious, and it was important to keep things light when we could. I'd seen them lose their composure plenty of times. I could count on Bette—a vet tech and a new mom struggling with some postpartum depression—to cry a couple of times a week, at least. Paisley was made of different stuff, and while she wasn't the sort to break down, I also felt an unspoken pact between us: *I'll be a rock if you'll be a rock*. I especially wouldn't let her see me lose my cool. I'd take a walk instead.

I took a final steadying breath and threw open my office door. "Heading out for a few," I said loudly, without making eye contact with anyone. I opened the main doors to the shelter and walked out onto Hacket Road. The heat hit me like a punch, as it always did when I left the air-conditioning. I'd lived in plenty of warm places—New Mexico, Texas, Southern California—but there was nothing like the dry desert heat of Modesto. So much for getting a breath of fresh air. Modesto was in California's Central Valley, a rural farming area, and was no Disneyland. Though it had some really nice attributes—such as the endless orchards I loved to run through—the town was mostly composed of strip malls. It was hit hard by the recession, and had high illiteracy and unemployment rates. To boot, it had earned the dubious distinction of being #1 in car theft in America. I missed San Diego, where I'd lived and worked before moving to Modesto, every single day.

How the hell did you get here, Kwane? And where the hell are you going?

The first question I knew the answer to, of course. My ex-wife was from Modesto and moved home after our divorce, taking our son, Kamon, with her. I wanted to be closer to him—he was just a baby when we split up, and growing so fast that even a couple of weeks away meant huge milestones missed. I'd tried living in San Jose and Carmel, both within a couple of hours of Modesto, but with unfulfilling work options. I'd tried commuting back and forth from Los Angeles and San Diego to Modesto, but the endless drives along much of the length of California got to be too much, and even with all the travel I didn't get to see Kamon as much as I wanted to.

It was when traveling to see Kamon that I'd come across the shelter. One afternoon while Kamon and I were out, my Doberman Belle managed to escape from the yard where I was staying and got hit by a car. She was taken to the Stanislaus County Animal Shelter, and after scanning her microchip, an employee called me to come in and retrieve her. Because I was a veterinarian, they asked if I wanted to go into the back and treat Belle, who had a fractured front leg, myself. To my amazement, the shelter did not have an in-house vet but the staff had done all they could to stabilize her. As I walked through the shelter, the curtain was pulled back and revealed a shocking scene. Dozens of poor animals were crammed into single cages, one after the other, and the decibel level was earsplitting. When I got to Belle I could tell immediately she was in pain and hadn't received proper care. I was so glad to get her out of there and get her home to treat her myself.

I didn't blame the staff; they were clearly doing the best they could with the resources they had. After I explained my current living situation to them, the director of the shelter practically begged me to come and run the place. I'd had years of experience in small clinics and was at one time the chief medical officer of the corporate chain Vetco, overseeing six hospitals and fifty vaccine clinics. Running a shelter was a whole other animal, though, pun intended, and definitely not my area of expertise. I turned her down but offered to help out with surgeries whenever I was in town. But in the ensuing weeks, I kept thinking about the possibility. I wanted to be closer to Kamon. I knew I could really help the shelter out. I needed to make a change, so took the job.

They'd been without a vet for two and a half years, and I'd never done anything like this in my life, so when I arrived my learning curve was steep. There were two big shocks right off the bat. One was working in a government position, which was totally new. There were so many rules and regulations I had to memorize. The other was the sound—constant dogfights I can only compare to the prison riots on *Oz*—and the smell—sewage, rust, mildew, and wet animal—which can only be described as a violent punch in the nose.

There were animals rolling in their own feces, sickly cats screeching, and dogs barking incessantly. The inmates were definitely running the asylum.

Caring for a large group of animals was a specialty in and of itself. I pored through texts, studies, and research to get up to speed. I set my own agenda and dove in. As cardboard boxes of kittens and canines were dumped on our doorstep, I performed as many spays and neuters as possible, up to twenty-five a day. I cared for hundreds of animals on site, and in my free time wrote new policies and procedures designed to decrease euthanasia and spike adoptions. Still, each morning I had to walk from kennel to kennel and, after a quick inspection, give the order to write the acronym on their ID cards that sentenced these unwanted animals to death.

I'd gone into survival mode and hardened my emotions to stay objective and focused, but I couldn't shake the nagging feeling that God was keeping track of how many animals I put down versus how many I saved. I was well aware of my unbalanced scorecard; I knew it was almost impossible to flip it, and it crushed me.

Only a couple years into the shelter job I was already feeling burned out, physically and emotionally, and had to drag myself into the office, despondent about my work and my life. I remembered my first furry shelter patient so vividly, Jasper, an affectionate green-eyed tabby given up after his owner's home foreclosed. But as time went on, there were too many to remember. Too many without names or histories. Too many that had never felt the touch of a compassionate owner, never felt safe, had never been treated kindly.

There was so much happening beneath the surface, so much trauma, in shelter work—for the animals *and* the staff. Personally,

I was suffering from severe compassion fatigue, and eventually my hard shell cracked into a million pieces. The panic attacks like the one I'd had that morning now came closer and closer together.

As I walked along Hacket Road, an industrial road with gas stations and a small airport, I thought about just getting into my car and leaving. I didn't ever have to go back in there. I could get a job with a vet hospital in town, or go back to San Diego and try commuting again. I probably had that same thought on a loop almost every day, and this day was no different.

Except, somehow, it was. I still had something to offer this place—I still thought I might be able to make it better, and I hadn't yet. I was too competitive to quit, though I wasn't sure who exactly I was competing against. I did know that if I left, Paisley, Bette, and the rest of the staff would be right back where they'd been the day Belle was brought in. No vet on staff, too many animals, no one who would dare stay long enough to see these huge problems through to actionable next steps and true solutions. It would feel like I'd abandoned them, like I'd abandoned the animals. I couldn't live with that. I just had to figure out how to stay while preserving my sanity. I had to find my way back to my life's purpose and calling. I had to find the love again, somehow.

* * *

The next day started just like the one before.

"Let's do this, Doc Stewy," Paisley said when I got in. She was ready with her clipboard and her resolve.

I sighed. "Another day, another dolla," I said.

"Oh, are you giving me a raise, then?"

"Sure, you know how deep these government pockets are. You're gonna be able to buy that yacht soon."

We walked the kennels and I started robotically giving the order to kill or not to kill—"Yes, no, no, no, no, yes, no." When we were about halfway through, I came upon a preemie Siamese kitten crouched in the dark back corner of her cage. She could fit in the palm of my hand and weighed less than a set of keys. Her mouth was covered in mucus and her eyes were so crusted with thick discharge I couldn't peel them open. She had clearly been starved for days and she was suffering. I immediately gave the order to euthanize her. I started to move to my right to the next cage, when out of the corner of my eye, I suddenly saw the kitten crawl blindly toward her food dish and start eating. The food dish that had been sitting there untouched since she arrived six hours earlier. It was a remarkable act. Most cats, when they are that sick and can't smell their food, won't go near it. There was something in this cat that wanted to survive.

That was the moment everything started to come together for me. I couldn't bring an emotional life into work—it was too painful, too exhausting. It's not like I'm the first veterinarian or even human being to feel this way. It's like when you read the paper or watch the news, but by the third page or first commercial you're numb. Refugees, mass death and illness, natural disasters—at some point you just need to turn it off, because it's too damn much. *What's the good of caring?* you think. *It's hopeless anyway, and what can I do?*

But there was a tiny life before me, and no, I couldn't save them all, but maybe I could save this one. Maybe it wasn't so simple as turning the spigot of suffering to full blast, or turning it off completely. Maybe I was inching closer to the answer I needed to survive in this work. "This is a fighter," I told Paisley. She looked at me and nodded. I paused. "Okay, don't do that one."

That night, though it was completely against my usual policy, I took the kitten home. I was worried she might be blind—her eyes were practically glued shut—so I gently massaged and held warm compresses on them. Not long after, her eyes finally popped open and pus ran out. I cleaned it up and put in some eye drops. When the infection had finally calmed enough for me to see her eyes clearly, they were swollen and blazing red. She had deep ulcers on her cornea and I thought her vision would never be normal. But within a week, the redness and cloudiness disappeared.

Kamon insisted on seeing her the second he came over. He held her and snuggled her and laughed his hilarious preschooler's laugh.

"Don't get attached," I told him. "She might not make it through this illness."

"She will," he said. He was obsessed, much like I'd been with the golden retriever when I was a few years older than him. And now I was in my mom's shoes.

"Well, even if she does, she needs to go back to the shelter," I warned.

"Okay, Daddy," he said, but even as he agreed I knew he wouldn't be okay with letting her go. I wasn't sure I would be, either.

Still, we had variations of this conversation every week as I nursed the kitten back to health. And each day, I grew more and more attached to her myself. Truth be told, I am not a cat person. Just like any other pet owner, vets have their favorites, too. Mine were big dogs. Plus, I'd never fostered any animals because I had created a strict rule about separating work and home life. At the shelter, when good Samaritans fostered animals, they'd often call us after a few weeks and say, "Actually, we've decided to keep him." My staff and I were always thrilled, and grateful, and when we hung up the phone we'd sing out, *"Suckers!"* with delight. I appreciated these suckers, but I was determined not to be one myself. I had too many animals to care for as it was.

But the kitten and I had formed that unexplainable bond between animal and human. Maybe I needed to let myself be a bit of a sucker. I'd cradled her in my arms as I held warm compresses on her eyes. I was there when her eyes finally opened for the first time. I felt her first purr vibrate on my chest.

After a month, she was finally big and healthy enough to be returned to the shelter and adopted. When I gathered her things together, Kamon started to cry.

"This was the plan all along," I explained to no avail and more tears.

"But I love her," he said.

"Are you going to take care of her?" I asked, already knowing that I had absolutely no resolve left.

"Yes. I'll take care of her," Kamon insisted.

Inside I was smiling. "Fine, we'll keep her."

"Let's name her Sushi!" he said. My favorite food.

Sushi became my cat, big and beautiful and brave. Every day this cat survived, every day she defied the odds, our bond grew. I gave her the unconditional love she deserved and she returned the favor. She cried for me in my absence and loved to perch on my shoulders first thing in the morning as I got ready for work. She was a true testament to survival. But also not really unique. What she taught me was that every pet that passed through our shelter was special. I couldn't save them all, but I couldn't make them faceless, either. It was okay to *see* them. I was loving them the best way I could.

Saving Sushi changed me profoundly and charged me with a new responsibility—to find as many opportunities as I could to be not a death dealer, but a *healer*. Once while she lay draped around my neck, soon after I had claimed her as my own, I whispered quietly to her, "Every animal I can save, I will." I had no idea of the journey this vow would take me on.

Chapter 2

A FEW BUCKS, A FEW MINUTES

The act of bullying was an art form when I was growing up in the '70s. It hadn't yet entered the popular psyche that maybe parents, teachers, and other kids should intervene when someone was getting picked on, so playgrounds were a free-for-all. Insults were strategically designed to hit where you were weakest, and adults didn't take much notice if a crowd of larger, more popular and self-assured kids gathered around one who looked different from all the others. They didn't realize, or didn't care, that kids can be ruthless.

I was the kid who looked different from all the others. My dad was Black, my mom white, and there weren't a lot of biracial kids in our small town in south Texas called, ironically, Brownsville. The town is close to the Mexican border, so there were plenty of Hispanic kids, but they all hung out together. I was in a social class no one understood, which made me an easy target. In second grade, I was the favorite of a group of boys in my class who hounded me merci-lessly, calling me "zebra." To my seven-year-old brain, it seemed like everything was working against me—the fact that I was biracial, the fact that I was skinny as hell, and that I was weird-looking. Add to that that my first name—Shannon—was a common name for a girl, and it felt like I was set up to fail.

"Are you Black or are you white?" asked one of my tormentors on the playground one day.

"Yeah, and are you a boy or are you a girl? What boy is called Shannon?" piped in another.

I held it together at school, usually. I'd come home, though, and bury my face in the fur of our Siamese mix cat, Miti. Her purr calmed me, and the way she nuzzled me made me feel loved, like she was happy to see me. One afternoon my dad—a football coach at the high school—asked what was wrong. "I hate my name," I said. "Everyone teases me. They tease me for *everything*."

Later that night he told my mom, "Sandy, Shannon's going away. We're going to start calling him by his middle name." I've been called Kwane ever since.

The bullying did not magically stop with the name change, unsur-prisingly. Nor did it stop when we moved to Albuquerque, where I was still one of the few biracial kids in class and still called "zebra." By middle school, I learned to talk back and talk shit. My mouth had learned to retaliate even if the rest of me hadn't. That didn't help things much, and those were the years I got beaten up the most. I vowed that one day, when I was bigger, I would get even.

By the time I got to high school, the overt bullying slowed, but something just as dark replaced it. I was often ignored. Overlooked.

I felt completely unseen—people just walked by me like I wasn't there. I don't know that people realize how painful it is to be ignored unless they've had that experience.

That's when I met Rob.

I'd known Rob vaguely since middle school, but never spoke to him until we were seated next to each other in freshman English. He wasn't exactly cool—he was a scrawny Mexican kid, not a strapping, clean-cut jock type. But he was wicked smart, like Matt Damon in *Good Will Hunting*. And he used that intelligence for good.

In English class one day, a girl passed me and said, "Geez, Kwane, my forearms are bigger than your legs. Eat some food, willya?"

I can't remember exactly what Rob said to her, but it was something about genetics and physiology that suggested I was a superior species and that she was the human equivalent of a bug. He straight-up *flattened* her. Everyone around us started laughing, but not at me. I thought, *Yeah, I'm gonna be friends with Rob.*

Rob and I hung out most of the rest of that year. When we were sophomores, Rob introduced me to some guys in the new freshman class he knew from middle school, and from then on, we were inseparable. We called ourselves the Blues Men, ostensibly because we liked the blues, but looking back on it, having a name for our group gave us a sense of belonging, of legitimacy. There were the twins, Chris and Craig—probably the coolest of the bunch of us, because they were tall and blond and had each other, but they were also super nerdy and would rather play Dungeons and Dragons than do anything else. There was Josh, a long-haired skater dude who ate only candy and looked like he could be blown down by a gust of wind. Dave was Asian in a place where Asians were even more of an anomaly than biracial kids like me. There was another Rob, the smartest of us all, who wore Coke-bottle glasses and who we called Rab so it would be less confusing. Scott was a redheaded, freckle-faced kid who was so small he made me look like Superman. On his own, Scott would have been shark bait. As part of the Blues Men, people left him alone.

At school, we'd cluster near the drama and speech classrooms, because a few of the guys were on the speech team. It was also near the edge of the school grounds, so we could self-isolate as much as we wanted. After school, we'd go to a spot along the Rio Grande few people knew about because you had to trek in. On the weekends, we'd lie to our parents about our whereabouts and would meet up by a liquor store. We'd bribe a homeless person to buy us alcohol and often take our purchase to an alley and share it with our "buyer." We had some great conversations in those days, with funny, cool people who found my group of nerdy friends funny and cool, too. When I started to work with the homeless decades later, I'd remember these nights and how some of my favorite people to hang out with back then were homeless—something that had never bothered me. The way I saw it then, we were all of us outcasts, just in different ways.

The friendship of the Blues Men pulled me out of loneliness for the first time in my life. I felt liberated to know that someone had my back. And it all started with Rob coming to my defense that day in freshman English. He could have looked straight ahead, or looked away. I might have, if I'd been him. But he chose to help me out and reached out his hand instead.

* * *

I regularly stopped at a 7-Eleven to get coffee on my way to work at the shelter, and a few times, I'd noticed a homeless guy sitting with his black pit bull mix. I usually avoided eye contact on my way into and out of the store. I was wary of engaging with the guy, guessing that he would probably ask me for something and I just didn't want to deal with it. It was easier to keep my eyes trained forward. But one day when I was coming out, I looked directly at the dog.

Huh, I thought, *hair loss, bumpy skin*. I can spot a case of flea allergy dermatitis (FAD) from ten feet away, and that's exactly what I saw when I looked at this dog. FAD is one of the more uncomfortable skin conditions that vets encounter. It's like having a rash or a second-degree burn, but all over the body. Dogs with FAD lose their hair, and their skin becomes red, raised, and bumpy. They don't know what's going on, obviously, just that they are extremely miserable, and they chew, scratch, and roll to try to get some relief, to no avail. Still, I didn't lock eyes with the owner or ask any questions. My plate was full, and it was easier to do nothing.

I kept thinking about this guy, though, and wondering what his story was. And I worried about his dog. I went back to the 7-Eleven the next day, and this time I made eye contact with the dog owner.

"Hey, how's it going?" I asked.

"Hey, man," he said.

"My name's Kwane—I'm a veterinarian, and it looks like your dog has some kind of allergy. Is he doing okay?"

"He's been scratching for months," said the guy. He introduced himself as Kyle, and his dog as Mutt. "He's miserable. He doesn't sleep, and so I don't sleep."

"If you're here in a day or so," I said, "I'll be back, and I'll bring you something for him."

I followed through, purchasing some medicine from the shelter with a few dollars from my wallet, and showing Kyle how to use it. "Once the fleas are dead, the skin will start to heal," I explained. "Give it two or three weeks."

A couple weeks later, I saw Kyle and Mutt again when I stopped for my coffee. Kyle smiled broadly as he greeted me. "It's a miracle," he said. "He's sleeping at night. I'm sleeping again. He's so much happier, he's wagging his tail all the time now. It's like he's a puppy again." Kyle started to cry. He clearly felt a strong responsibility for and connection to Mutt, and wanted to do right by him. He must have felt so helpless all those months, knowing his dog was uncomfortable and not being able to fix it. Worse yet, scores and scores of people walked by, completely oblivious to his predicament. I think the only thing worse than feeling unseen would be needing help and still feeling unseen. I don't know for sure, but I think that through our exchange, this man saw hope and humanity after being ignored for so long by the community around him—including me.

As I drove in to work that day, I didn't feel self-congratulatory. In fact, I felt a little guilty. It was so easy—just a few bucks out of my pocket and a few minutes out of my time, and look how much happier this man was, look at how much more comfortable his dog was. Why had it taken me so long to make a connection with him?

I checked in on Kyle again, but in the weeks that followed I also found myself pulling my car over whenever I saw a homeless person with a pet. Later, a social worker informed me it's insensitive to use the word *homeless*. That I should say "people experiencing homelessness" instead. Later still, someone pointed out that it's not that they don't have a home, it's that they don't have a house and that I should call them houseless. In my view, and in conversations I've had with them, it doesn't much matter to them. What matters is that I'm helping out.

Abandoned parking lots, underpasses, and canal banks became usual stopping points for me, as I talked to people and handed out medications, advice, and peace of mind. I treated ear infections, overgrown toenails, flea infestations, and eye conditions. I connected with each person, and I connected with each animal. It was a complete antidote to my rounds with Paisley. I got to see myself as a healer again, and it did wonders for my soul. In working with the homeless population, I felt like I was coming back to life.

Things were getting better at the shelter, too. When I'd first arrived, it was triage all the time. We had six animal control officers working full time, being dispatched around the county to pick up strays, roadkill, and animals that had been hit by cars. I'd arrive some mornings and, before I could even get started on my rounds, I'd have to deal with the emergencies that had come in during the night. I felt like I just couldn't get ahead of it, I couldn't take a step back and breathe, let alone think about ways to not just stanch the bleeding, but prevent it. Working with the homeless population, I met advocates who were coming up against the same struggles. Sure, they could get someone off the street for a night, but that was a Band-Aid, not a meaningful solution. In both arenas, long-standing problems needed to be addressed in ways that would make things easier, because the status quo just led to frustration and burnout.

In time, though, I became more comfortable handling the crises around me at the shelter so that I could carve out small periods of time to think and to strategize. I called brainstorming meetings with staff, and with the county board of supervisors, and we began earmarking money for programs that would make a meaningful difference.

My first system-wide intervention involved the overpopulation of cats, a serious problem. Like tigers in the wild, cats are wired to "hold" their territory by keeping others out of it. So when you have too many cats in a square mile, you have catfights galore, and the spreading of disease. Not to mention the dozens of kittens that were dropped off at the shelter—too young to adopt out, too needy for us to be able to care for. The prevailing wisdom to control the feline population up until then had been to trap and euthanize unwanted cats. But the prevailing wisdom didn't work: If you left one male cat and one female cat around, they'd become super breeders. On an instinctual level they understood their population was under threat, and so they repopulated many areas very quickly, and the catfights, disease spread, and unwanted kittens continued. To combat this, I implemented a program called TNR—Trap, Neuter, Return. If we neutered cats and placed them back where we'd found them, they'd hold their territory, and there would be no more excessive breeding.

I also led efforts to advocate for a new shelter. The Stanislaus County Animal Shelter was long overdue for a reboot, and once I'd gained the trust of the community, I argued to the county council that we were a statewide embarrassment (though I refrained from using exactly those words). I knew that for shelters to lower their kill rates, they needed to be warm, welcoming spaces where members of the community would want to spend time, whereas everything about the existing shelter said "run the hell away." With the approval of the council, we broke ground on a new facility. I lobbied hard for the facility to include a spay-and-neuter clinic that we'd let local veterinarians operate out of for free, in exchange for them performing spays and neuters for us at a low cost. We would ultimately be able to pump through hundreds of spays and neuters that would not have been done if not for this program.

Our shelter design also had indoor and outdoor spaces where pet-seekers could spend time with potential adoptees, without fear that Leatherface would come through with a chain saw at any moment. We had large exercise runs, so the dogs weren't cooped up all day. Every dog and cat had its own kennel, which dramatically reduced fights and disease spread. Whereas before the staff had spent enormous time and energy treating contagious diseases such as distemper and parvovirus, now we had more bandwidth to take better care of the animals, and of ourselves. I had an office with a proper desk, and a window that looked out onto a pasture, whereas before I'd been in a corner of a converted cafeteria. Paisley and Bette had desks, too, instead of sharing a table surrounded by cinder-block walls. We were revived. We felt better, more energetic.

Because of programs like TNR, the spay/neuter clinic, and the more welcoming shelter environment, we were able to drop our euthanasia rate. When I began working there, the "live release rate," or number of animals who left the facility to new homes versus being euthanized, was under 40 percent. Through a combination of the Trap, Neuter, Return program and a new facility that made the shelter an integral part of the community, by the time I left, the live release rate was nearing 75 percent. The trend continued, and I'm told it's happily now 97 percent. Almost all of these animals would find a home.

I hardly did any of this alone. It was a group effort, and one that continues. But I was undoubtedly one of the effort's leaders. And no way could I have stuck it out without Sushi, and Kyle, and Rob in my mind reminding me that no person or animal needs to be invisible.

Chapter 3

SKID ROW

As the shelter became stronger, I felt that I could resign without leaving Paisley and Bette with a mess. The war might not be over, but we'd won some epic battles and it felt like V-day was coming. What's more, I was approached with a job opportunity I couldn't say no to: leading the "No Animals Were Harmed" program for American Humane. Essentially, I'd get to hang out on film sets and make sure the animals were treated fairly, and get to know their trainers and how they ran their businesses. The work was exciting and low-stress, and after five grueling years at the shelter, I needed it.

I began spending more and more time in Los Angeles for the new job, and after I'd spend a day in the magic of Hollywood, around catered lunch tables piled high with club sandwiches and quinoa-avocado salads, I'd drive to the apartment I'd rented and notice the stark contrast on the gritty streets of West Hollywood. A block after multimillion-dollar homes, there'd be a block of tents and busted-up RV campers. As I had in Modesto, I began stopping and talking to the homeless people who had pets, asking if their animals needed anything. It's a truism that once you start noticing something, you notice it everywhere—and that felt on the nose for the homeless population. It's like I'd had blinders on before and now had a range of vision that spotted every sleeping-bag-piled shopping cart on the side of the road.

I started spending some evenings and a lot of weekends actively seeking out places where I could make an impact. From Venice Beach to Manhattan Beach, and from West Hollywood to Skid Row, there were more people with pets than I could possibly help. But I took the approach that doing something was better than doing nothing. And conversation by conversation, I got an education about homelessness in America. Or, rather, a reeducation.

I had long thought that to end up living on the street, you had to have really messed up somewhere in life. Maybe you were lousy with money, or crappy with relationships, or had a drug or alcohol problem you couldn't get under control. I chalked people's predicament up to some bad luck and some weaknesses in character. It's not that I spent a lot of time sitting around being judgmental of the homeless—the truth is I just didn't think much at all beyond the obvious about why they'd come to live that way.

My first trip to Skid Row shocked me. Skid Row is a neighborhood of Los Angeles where, since the 1970s, the homeless have been legally permitted to set up camp. The area's roots go further back, though—it's been a gathering place for those down on their luck for nearly a hundred years. Skid Row now covers fifty city blocks and has a population in the thousands. The sheer size of it overwhelmed me, as did its proximity to some of the more glamorous sections of

Los Angeles. Broken-down cars sit in the middle of the street, and no one tows them away. It smells of urine that's been baked in the sun, and in the event the wind gusts, you catch a whiff of rotting food and sewage. You'll hear people shouting at each other from across the street, or you'll catch bits and pieces of an escalating argument a block away—it sounds a bit like being at a rowdy football game. It's not complete lawlessness—it's not like there are people out shooting and stabbing one another—but it feels chaotic and rough. It feels like you need to be hyperaware of what's going on around you, and to be prepared to get in a defensive stance if you need to.

It was on Skid Row that I met Walter, an older Black man who walked with a limp, spoke with a mumble, and whose health issues had kept him on the streets for several years. Building trust with him was painstaking. Like a lot of homeless people I meet, he was leery of strangers like me offering to help him and his pet. How did he know I wasn't going to take his dog, Dinker, away? He'd heard stories of other people this had happened to. I'd heard those stories, too. I once got a frantic call from a woman living on the streets whose pit bull I'd seen just a week before. She said animal control had taken her dog because she couldn't show proof of a rabies vaccine. When she went to try to get her dog out of the shelter, they wouldn't return him to her because she couldn't show ID. And even if she did have ID, she still didn't have the money or wherewithal to figure out his rabies documentation.

I called the shelter on the woman's behalf and determined that the dog was really stressed—he wouldn't come out of the corner and wouldn't eat. They said that when the seven-day hold for his owner to reclaim him expired, he'd be eligible for adoption. But he probably wouldn't be adopted because he wouldn't come out of the corner. "He doesn't show well," they said.

"Of course he doesn't show well!" I shouted. "He's not a show dog! He's traumatized and he's missing his owner. He hasn't been apart from her for a minute of his life."

If this dog that "didn't show well" wasn't adopted, he would be placed on a list for possible euthanasia. All of this suffering just because the owner couldn't produce documentation for a vaccine that the shelter could easily have administered. I'm not the kind of guy who gets worked up (anymore), but I was livid. I was embarrassed, too, because it was incidents like this that gave shelters a bad name. And look, I understood they were dealing with a lot of dogs, and it's not impossible something like this happened when I was at the Stanislaus County Animal Shelter. When you have massive systems, cases slip through the cracks. But it also shouldn't have taken six calls from me to get it straightened out. At least there was a happy ending, because eventually, I got the right person on the phone and the dog was returned to his owner.

All of this is to say, I understood why Walter was so fearful of my intervention. He didn't want some high-and-mighty doctor thinking he knew better than Walter what was good for Dinker. He knew that if he lost his dog to a massive system, it would be harder than hell to get him out. So Walter wanted to see my business card, my website, and to learn everything he could about me.

I sat next to him on the curb and showed him my business card. "Do you know what the DVM after my name stands for?" I asked.

"Yeah," said Walter. "Damn Vet Motherfucker!"

I laughed, and then he laughed. And then I felt like there was this bond, a little glimmer of trust between us.

I assured him I wouldn't take Dinker anywhere unless Walter came too, and asked him if I could examine him right there. Dinker was black and white, around sixty pounds, with floppy ears and warm brown eyes that seemed to pick up on every movement or feeling from Walter. As I examined him I saw something really unusual, something I'd never seen before in all my time as a vet. Dinker had an extremely rare condition called hypospadias, in which the opening of the urethra is on the underside of the penis instead of at the tip. Hypospadias is uncomfortable—it made it hard for Dinker to relieve himself completely. Hypospadias also makes urinary tract infections more common.

It was one of the more serious conditions I'd seen in my street work, and with Walter's permission, I brought in my friend Antonio Pedraza, a highly sought-after veterinary surgeon, to come have a look. We laid Dinker on a picnic table near Walter's tent in order to examine him. Walter held Dinker from behind, both his arms wrapped around the dog, and buried his head in Dinker's neck. Walter was so overwhelmed by the prospect that there was something really wrong with Dinker that he cried into the animal's coat during most of the examination.

"This isn't a sad moment," Dr. Pedraza said, gently. "It's a good moment to understand what is going on with him. We don't want to stress you."

"I don't want to lose him," Walter said into Dinker's neck. "He's all I got."

I told Walter that Dinker wasn't going anywhere, but that it would be good to understand more about what was going on with him. Walter agreed to come with us to a vet clinic where we could do a full ultrasound and get a urine sample. But when it came to the X-ray we wanted, Walter wasn't having it. He was fine with Dinker getting the X-ray, but he wasn't okay with Dinker being out of his sight—which, to protect Walter from radiation exposure, he would have to be.

"I can't let him go by himself," Walter said. "I can't, I can't, I won't."

The fear and desperation in Walter's voice were unmistakable. Still, we needed to get an accurate picture of what was going on with this dog and how we could help him. My challenge was to put Walter at ease, to earn his confidence as well as I could so that we could help Dinker. I figured out a way that Walter could *watch* the X-ray from a safe distance. He said he would be okay with that—he didn't need to be touching Dinker, but he needed to be able to see him.

Walter had just been screwed over too many times in his life. I believe Walter liked me and Dr. Pedraza, but how could we undo a lifetime of people saying one thing and doing another? Decades of people actually *not* having good intentions when it came to Walter? His brain was wired to see threat everywhere, and a few hours with well-meaning people couldn't rewrite his history. But there was even more to Walter's reluctance. His relationship with his animal was one of intense codependence—they hadn't been apart from each other since Walter had rescued Dinker from a dumpster when he was a puppy. I never learned Walter's whole story, but he had clearly not had an easy life. So far as I could tell, he didn't have a family, or even friends. His dog brought him joy, affection, and a sense of home. To suggest that Walter was attached to Dinker doesn't go far enough—he *needed* that dog.

In the end, Walter would not let me and my team operate on Dinker. He was too fearful of the risks of the anesthesia. It sucked, because I knew Walter was going to lose Dinker anyway, probably to a urinary tract infection. And I wasn't sure Walter could survive without Dinker, so feared losing them both. But as much as I wanted to help, it wasn't my place to push the surgery on Walter. With all of my clients, the owner makes the call—whether that owner lives on Rodeo Drive or Skid Row, they still deserve respect for their decision-making. Their story was theirs to write, and all I could do was provide guidance, some medication to help manage Dinker's pain, some antibiotics to stop infections, and my phone number in case Walter changed his mind. He never called.

* * *

One of the next people I met on Skid Row was a young woman named Susan. She was camped out with her dog, Biloxi—a mutt who bore an uncanny resemblance to Toto from *The Wizard of Oz*. Susan had bright blue eyes behind the red rims of her glasses, and with her nose stud, messy bun, and bohemian-chic style, she looked like someone who would ordinarily be teaching yoga on Sunset, not setting up a tent on Skid Row. She already knew the pros and cons of the various vaccines I'd suggested for Biloxi, had already weighed her choices, and had already had him vaccinated on a careful schedule. I was curious to get her story, and Biloxi's.

Susan had moved from Minnesota to LA and was just a few credits shy of getting her master's degree in social work when she lost her job, and then her apartment. After maxing out her credit cards, she was too proud to ask for a bailout from her family or go back home. She thought she'd live in her car until she landed on her feet. A year later, the car was gone, her credit cratered below 400, and she was still homeless.

"I thought I knew what being homeless might be like," she said. "But you can't really know until you're pushing a shopping cart with all your stuff in it." She held her fingers an inch apart. "You feel this small."

Hers was a refrain I'd hear over and over again.

"This is not me."

"I don't want to be here."

"I still can't believe this is my life."

"I used to have a house."

"I used to have a boat."

"Many homeless people are smarter than you would believe," said Pudge, who had been a wrestling coach before he ended up on the streets. "I've talked to ex-lawyers and ex-judges, former professional ball players." He said one thing or another happens—the end of a relationship, divorce, or bad luck—and you lose it all.

I met people who had been doing okay—even well—in their lives, but then an illness combined with crappy insurance—or no insurance—bankrupted them. Or others who were saddled with loans from their student days, and the job market didn't support them like they'd hoped. Or others who had lost their homes to natural disasters. With poor credit, and the high cost of living in a competitive housing market, they didn't feel they had a choice but to move into their car—just for a while. But then, once they fell through the net, they couldn't climb back up to a place of stability.

The truth is, it freaked me out a bit. *There but for the grace of God go I* had been an oft-repeated mantra in my house growing up. *Don't judge, lest you be judged.* I'd heard the words but never felt them until I got up close and personal to these people's stories. I thought back to my own near misses. Though I'd made it to the prestigious veterinary school at Colorado State University, I came close to derailing my future by almost flunking out. I dug myself out of the academic hole by my fingernails, only to nearly get a DUI a few months later.

It was unbelievably stupid. I'd just finished finals and had gone out drinking with a group of vet school friends. I'd learned plenty from my dad about getting pulled over as a Black man in America. I did everything he'd taught me: hands on the dash where the officer could see them. Calm voice. Be respectful, call him "officer." But nothing could cover over the fact that I was drunk. When the officer asked me to follow a penlight with my eyes, and I couldn't, I blustered that I must have mystagmus—a random piece of medical knowledge I learned for my finals, that meant your eyes flutter left to right when you have certain diseases or impairments. He asked how I knew what that was, and I explained I was a student of veterinary medicine.

"Hm," he said. "Okay." I don't think he bought that I actually had mystagmus, but he let me go. He told me to drive straight home and go to bed.

My conversations in Skid Row brought the memory to the surface, and thoughts of it haunted me. What if he had given me a DUI? It would have gone on my record just at the time I was entering the job market—not exactly a selling point. Not to mention I couldn't have gotten to my interviews without a license. What if my DUI kept me from getting hired? I'd always been able to secure housing based on my student status, but what would have happened when I wasn't a student anymore? My credit would tank. Of course, unlike a lot of people living on Skid Row, I had a good relationship with my parents. But I'm not sure I'd have been able to stomach asking them if I could live with them—not as a guy in my mid-twenties. Like Susan, I probably would have been too proud.

I played it out. I could have crashed with friends until I landed a job. I could have taken a job I didn't want or that I was overqualified for. But then what? The poor pay, stacked against the student loans, compounded by how shitty I would feel about myself for screwing up my golden ticket—ugh. Yeah, I couldn't imagine living on Skid Row, but I also *could*.

There but for the grace of God go I.

* * *

I was spending a lot of time thinking about animal behavior and training because of my new day job working on movie sets. Observing those Hollywood animals gave me a deep level of respect and appreciation for their intelligence and—no kidding—their work ethic. I was on commercial sets with bears who would do anything for a Hershey chocolate treat. I was on sets with lions whose majestic presence gave me chills. But the stories I thought of most were usually those of dogs. I was struck, watching them work on set, how *happy* they seemed to be doing the same shots over and over again. They didn't ever seem to tire, and they carried themselves with unmistakable pride. They wanted to please their trainers, and they wanted to please the actors they were working with. (Incidentally, the bonding between an animal and the actor it works with is taken very seriously. Just as you would expect directors to want to build chemistry between romantic leads, they very much care about building chemistry between actor and animal actor.)

On set, I saw dogs that were happy, proud, and extremely connected to their humans.

On the streets, I saw the exact same thing.

In truth, the connection between homeless people and their pets is on a totally different level, and that's one of the first things that challenged my preconceived ideas about the homeless.

With each new animal I helped, I gained a deeper understanding of this unique bond. I saw homeless people feed their pet before they fed themselves. I saw them give their last dollar to care for their pet. They sustained each other. I can't tell you how many times people told me their animals were their reason for getting up in the morning. As with Dinker and Walter, I saw that these pets provided more than companionship to their owners—they also offered love, hope, and security.

Even in their darkest moments, the homeless people I met had their loyal companions by their sides. Homeless people are loving, dedicated pet owners—which I hadn't thought the case before I started my work. Maybe you've seen a homeless person sitting on the ground outside a store with a dog sitting obediently next to them, and your first reaction was, "Oh, that poor animal!" It shouldn't be. Not only do the homeless usually adopt animals from shelters or take in strays, they're with them 24/7. To a pet, their owner is their universe. But we go to work and leave our pets alone sometimes eight, ten, twelve hours a day and they just sit and pine for us. Homeless pets, in contrast, get plenty of exercise and fresh air.

The second thing that surprised me was how well behaved the animals I met were. From my days in private practice, I was used to unruly pets—particularly dogs. But on the streets the animals were almost angelic. On the private clinic side of things, almost every day I'd have an owner come in pulled entirely by their animal. "I have no control," I remember one lady telling me about her 70-pound golden retriever. And she was right. He was a ball of energy who barked at people and other dogs, completely ignored his owner, and urinated in the lobby. I asked her what training she'd tried, and she shrugged. "I've taken him to a few classes, but things are just so busy. It's hard to be consistent about it all." Hers is a familiar story. I can't tell you the number of times I've cautioned, "If you don't have the time for a dog: Do. Not. Get. A. Dog." I'm not shy about it.

But on the streets, it was almost eerie how well behaved the dogs were—perhaps precisely because the owners had time. I still always, always advocate having a dog on a leash, but even if the owners hadn't had their dogs leashed (almost all did), the dogs would have stayed put. The animals were so accustomed to being around other people, they usually didn't bark or growl when I approached. They weren't reactive around other dogs. They could read their owner's body language because they were so connected and spent so much time together. An owner could quietly say, "Snoopy, sit still for the doctor," and I swear the animal understood. A young woman named

Precious suffered random seizures on the street. But she was so in sync with her Chihuahua Chico de Barge ("it's like I birthed him myself"), the pup learned to warn her when a seizure was imminent with a howl that "sounds like a fire truck siren."

The third thing that struck me was the "extended family" atmosphere of many homeless tent cities. I've seen homeless people be cursed at, have things thrown at them, and be treated just abysmally. Because of that, the homeless community is like an invisible fortress. There is a shared humanity and an amazing bond within the homeless community itself. There was a harshness to their living conditions, obviously, but also a compassionate connection among neighbors. Which I thought was poignant, considering so many homeless people were often rejected, abused, or neglected by their real families, the reason they ended up on the street in the first place. For instance, I met this guy Knuckles—named so because of the knuckleball he threw back in his baseball days. Knuckles didn't have a dog himself, but he directed me to people a mile either side of him who did, and whose pets he knew needed some help. When I found them, I'd say, "Knuckles said you might need some help." Their faces lit up. "Knuckles! How is that guy anyway?"

I didn't tell my dad about the street work. I didn't tell my mom, either, or my brother, Ian, who I'm really close to. They know about it now, of course, and Ian is a key part of my street work. But for a long time I was really quiet about my volunteer work, even as I began spending more and more of my time on Skid Row. I loved that street work was *my* thing, my secret. When I was a kid, whenever I fantasized about becoming something other than a vet, I imagined myself as a superhero. I think part of me was living out that childhood fantasy, Bruce Wayne by day, hobnobbing with the Los Angeles rich and famous on Hollywood sets, and Batman by night.

At some point, however, I realized I couldn't fund all the vaccinations, supplies, and surgery needs myself or call in favors constantly. So I began some low-key fundraising. To attract more donors, Ian and I decided to film some short episodes of me doing my street work, and that footage became a show called *The Street Vet*, and we started a nonprofit with the same name. The work wasn't private anymore—I was no longer Batman out doing my thing in secret. To my surprise, the involvement of others only made the work more satisfying, because it turned out a lot of people wanted to help.

That said, when I did start sharing my work with others, I got some pushback. "You should seize their animals," people have said to me. "They're not in a position to be able to care for them!" They might well point to a story like Walter and Dinker's as evidence. But what do they think would have happened to Dinker, if not for Walter? He would have surely died as a puppy. The homeless aren't on waiting lists for desired breeds; they're taking the least desirable animals who would likely die without a human caring for them. And, I follow up, should I seize the animal, where would I take it? To the shelter? Of all people, I knew all too well what shelters had in store for animals like Dinker. No, Dinker was right where he should be.

And walking around the streets in my scrubs, I realized, so was I.

Chapter 4

GO GET YOURSELF
A DOG

When I attended the University of New Mexico, I lived in a tiny, 580-square-foot apartment right off campus with my buddy Mike, and we shared bunk beds because our room was so small. Notwithstanding our bed setup, I felt like a grown-up for the first time in my life—I was doing my own laundry, cooking for myself, inviting people over without having to check with anyone. Mike and I became tight, despite the fact that I was a milk-loving guy who also happened to be lactose intolerant. To this day he tells me he has early onset dementia because of my gas in those years.

We had a great time, but I felt like something key to my life was missing, and it was. For the first time, I had no responsibility for an animal. I didn't have a pet. My whole life, I'd been the one primarily in charge of caring for the family's pets, and so I always considered them *mine*. But recently my mom had gotten into breeding Russian wolfhounds, or borzois—the big, regal-looking dogs you see on vodka bottles. At the end of my high school years, she'd transitioned from breeding the dogs to showing them all around the Southwest and Midwest. I was old enough to stay home as she traveled from dusty town to dusty down, but Ian was only nine, and went everywhere with my mom and the dogs. My mom bought him a snazzy clip-on tie and fancy vest, and pushed the poor kid into the ring like he was a character out of *Best in Show*.

My mom's new obsession meant that our family dogs felt like *her* dogs, not mine. If I got on the floor with one of them and started to tussle with it, she'd say, "Don't do that, Kwane, it will change his behavior in the ring."

At the end of my sophomore year in college, my desire for my own dog had grown to the point of distraction. Now I realize why—I've read all the data about how animals reduce stress, that they alleviate anxiety and lower blood pressure. I didn't know any of these benefits of pet companionship at the time, I just knew that when an animal was around me, I felt better. Growing up, if I'd had a hard day at school, or didn't place well in a race, or dealt with bullying from other kids, I'd come home and nuzzle our cat, Miti, or one of our dogs would put its head in my lap, and I'd feel better. I would talk to them all the time, like they were a brother or a sister. My pets were my solace. Now when I was stressed, or sad, or just low, I didn't have my go-to coping mechanism of animal companionship.

I figured, I'm an adult now, cooking for myself, cleaning for myself. Why shouldn't I get a dog?

To be clear, it was a terrible idea, and one my mom tried to talk me out of. College is not the ideal time to get a dog. Parties, irregular hours, long absences, and tons of different short-term housing situations just do not make for a good lifestyle for dog ownership. Dogs are expensive, and students don't exactly have a lot of extra income. Sometimes it's all you can do in college to keep *yourself* healthy and breathing, so it doesn't make sense to bring a dog into the mix. Still, right after I finished my sophomore year, Mike and I lucked into a house rental, and I got my first Doberman, Baron.

I didn't think it through at all. All I knew was that the house had a yard. It had actually once been a fraternity house, but when the frat was disbanded the owner decided to rent to a group of six guys— reassured by us that we would be an improvement over the last group. We told him that we were responsible, that we would take good care of the house, and that no, of course we didn't have any pets. As soon as we signed the lease, I opened up the paper and started searching the classifieds for puppies for sale.

I'd long been obsessed with Dobermans, and found an ad where there were three left. I'd been working as a Domino's delivery driver, and stuffed my tip money in the ashtray of the old pickup truck I drove. I had just enough—$130—to buy the last male they had, a black-and-tan puppy I named Baron after a grocery store billboard I saw on our inaugural ride home.

Baron and I were tight. He was *my* dog. He'd sleep on my bed every night, and as he grew—he was nearly 90 pounds—he grew more protective of me. Once a good friend of mine, Ivar, came into my room and sat on the edge of my bed while I was sleeping, and Baron went after him.

"Baron, it's me!" Ivar soothed, but still backed away. "Fine, I get it," Ivar said. "Don't mess with Dad while he's sleeping."

Life felt right again now that I had a dog. Pet ownership reinvigorated me, and renewed my passion for animals, and my determination to be a vet one day.

Baron saw a lot of people and other dogs, and was great with all of them. He would hang out at our parties—he was a party dog, and I can't say I'm proud of that. Baron also tormented my roommates. He barked constantly, tore up the yard, scratched up the fence. He ate shoes and baseball caps and whatever food was within reach. He was a typical puppy and not getting nearly enough stimulation, because I was in class all day, then at track practice, and then often away for meets. My roommates loved him and helped out, but he was a lot to handle—especially for my high school buddy Josh, the skinny skater kid who was one of the Blues Men. Josh's room was right next to mine, and it had once been a sleeping porch. With its turf in place of carpet, it had the sense of a semi-outdoor space even though it was fully enclosed. Baron decided semi-outdoor was close enough, and would routinely carry out his morning bathroom routine in the middle of Josh's room.

One morning I woke up to hear Josh cursing in the yard. He was holding his boxers up on his skinny frame with one hand, while brandishing our fireplace poker in the other. "God damn it, Baron!" he shouted as he chased Baron around the yard. "God damn it!" I just laughed—Josh was a teddy bear who would never hurt an animal. But there's no doubt he was furious.

Josh forgave Baron, though, and he forgave me. But even though I can't imagine *not* having had Baron, it wasn't a great life for a puppy.

When I left the University of New Mexico for vet school in Colorado Springs, Baron was right by my side in my truck, while my dad drove another car of stuff behind me. I blasted music, one hand on my dog, the other on the steering wheel, and felt invincible. My life was made. I had my own dog, and I was going to the best vet school in the nation.

My dad stayed a couple of days to get me settled, then took me to Key Bank to set up my first checking account before he left. I was twenty-two years old and still didn't have a bank account. My dad said goodbye in that Key Bank parking lot, and it suddenly hit me that this was it—I was leaving home. My eyes started welling up, and my dad grabbed my shoulder and said, "Look at me! This is good! This is going to be good." I nodded, then looked over at Baron's head sticking out my truck's window. *Yeah,* I thought, and shook off the emotion. *It'll be good.*

* * *

Konrad Lorenz is considered a founder of the field of animal behavior, and author of the classic *Man Meets Dog.* In the book, he offers some guesses about why our wild-man ancestors began to domesticate the dog some 50,000 years ago. "At the approach of evening, the dread of the coming night began to weigh heavy on every mind; they were obsessed by that fear of the unknown . . ." Lorenz imagines a clan leader recognizing that the howling of jackals who followed the camp was not just an annoyance but a sort of rough alarm system. Their alertness to oncoming predators made them useful, so when the camp moved on, the clan leader threw the creatures a bone or scrap of meat so they'd follow. The clan members could then close their eyes and rest at night, knowing that the animals had their backs.

Looked at this way, we've had alarm systems for 50,000 years, and even technology today can't beat the oldest version. I've heard police tell people, "Forget alarm systems—they can be disengaged. Get yourself a dog."

"The whole charm of the dog," Lorenz wrote, "lies in the depth of the friendship and the strength of the spiritual ties with which he has bound himself to man." Lorenz wrote this more than half a century before scientific studies were searchable online, and he would have been happy to see how the science agrees with him. For starters—and I'll try not to get too geeky here, because I can go on for ages—the more affectionate you are with your dog, the higher your oxytocin levels (a hormone that's associated with things like empathy and trust) and the lower your cortisol (your stress hormone). As your levels change, so do your dog's, an example of how they mirror you. Another study showed that people turned to their dogs for comfort not quite as much as they turned to their mothers or sisters, but more than they turned to their fathers or brothers. It's on the strength of research like this—and, frankly, common sense and observation—that dogs became used as service dogs, therapy dogs, and emotional support dogs. This bond is why dogs are used in nursing homes and in children's wards in hospitals, why dogs are used to help treat PTSD in veterans, and why they are increasingly used to help with anxiety. In *The New Work of Dogs*, the journalist Jon Katz puts it this way: "Every dog is descended from creatures who aided primitive, frightened humans when they most needed it. Today, when we are less primitive but still frightened, they are working harder than ever."* And not just dogs, either. Horses have long been used for therapeutic

---

* Jon Katz, *The New Work of Dogs* (New York: Villard, 2003), 26.

riding—there are even references to it in ancient Greek literature. Birds—as you'll see when you meet Barbara in a later chapter—can offer enormous comfort, and, as Sushi proves, so do cats.

I learned a lot about animals' capabilities to help humans while I was in vet school, I've certainly observed it time and time again, but I also lived it. Sushi came into my life at a time when I felt broken and needed a little hope and healing. But before I was ever a cat guy, I was a die-hard dog guy. My family had a Doberman when I was half the dog's size, and I worshipped at the altar of that animal, or so I'm told—I was too young to have solid memories of him. But we got another Doberman when I was in high school, and that's why in college I chose Baron.

People do get hooked on specific breeds—I've seen it happen again and again, where someone will fall in love with a dog, a Wheaton terrier, for instance, whose breed is actually not super convenient for their lifestyle, but no matter—they are Wheaton terrier people to the death. That was me with Dobermans. They are a beautiful animal— their athleticism makes them wondrous to watch when they stretch out into a full run. I loved their silky coats, pointy ears, and undeniable intelligence. Seriously, Dobermans rank as the fifth-smartest breed (just behind golden retrievers, which I find strange because goldens always seem a little hapless to me). Their scary exterior belies their gentle ways, and you'll never meet a dog as loving as a Doberman, or as tolerant to sticky toddler fingers pulling at their coats.

When Kamon's mom and I split up, we had two Dobermans, Belle and Solomon. For the first few years, I was on the move so much—commuting back and forth to Modesto from wherever I was working—that it made sense for them to stay with my ex more often than not. I also liked to think they provided some stability and comfort to Kamon.

It was a rocky period in my life, marked by long hours on the road, a lot of stress and uncertainty, and an overarching sense of transience. I missed my son, and I missed my dogs—especially Solomon. He was my big, beautiful specimen of a dog, so intelligent, obedient, and attentive. I can't fully explain it, nor could I make a case in a court of law or anything, but Solomon just *got* me. He was *my* dog. My ex understood this—she said every time I came home, it seemed to take years off his life and he became a puppy again. He would circle around me and prance by my side, incessantly. Remember how Buddy the Elf acted around his dad, once he learned he had one? That was Solomon with me, and even for someone who spent day in and day out surrounded by animals, the closeness and attention of this animal that was undeniably "for me" felt pretty good.

When I greeted the dogs after a long separation, Belle would excitedly lick my face for a minute, but then wander off. Solomon, though, would stay by my side. It's like we were acknowledging to each other that we needed some one-on-one time, that we needed to connect. I'd sit on the floor with him, and we would just look into each other's eyes. I swear I understood everything he was saying to me with his warm and intelligent brown eyes: *I see you, and I see your sadness. When are you coming back? When are we going to be together all the time again?*

I'd rub his head, pet his long black-and-tan body, put my arms around his broad chest, then look him in the eye again for our next round of voiceless communication. *It's hard right now. It's going to be okay. I'm glad you're here.*

I couldn't be with Solomon all the time, and yet he was always, *always* there for me. I still think of what it meant to me. And even though I was going through a bumpy stretch, it was nothing compared to what some people go through. That period of time with Solomon, and the value I took from his comfort and devotion, gave me a deep appreciation for the role animals play in the lives of the people I meet on the streets.

* * *

San Diego has miles of sandy beaches and an average of 266 sunny days a year, so it's not surprising that it's drawn the fourth-highest homeless population in the United States. Drive around a little bit and it's not hard to find encampments—sometimes you'll find a row of broken-down RVs, but more often, you'll see clusters of tents. They pop up along the highway, on some downtown streets, and in parks. One afternoon, making rounds in the hilly park by the San Diego Zoo, I met a skater named Skye. She wore her baseball cap backwards, and a large hoodie and jeans. She and her mom had a tent pitched and had been living in the park for a couple of months with their young mutt, Lexi.

The rest of what I learned about Skye came out slowly, and over time. She was maybe five feet tall, with short-cropped blond hair, a big smile, and a shy, awkward way that reminded me of middle schoolers I'd met. She told me she was eighteen, but I don't always get the full story or the truth. Skye looked very much like a kid to me.

If she was underage, it would be illegal for a child to be living on the streets and I would be required to report her to the police. So she had every reason to lie to me—I didn't hold it against her.

If Skye was reluctant to share much about herself, she was a lot more forthcoming about Lexi. "She's a nuisance," she said, but it was clear the two were tight. Skye's biggest complaint was that no matter how many chew toys she offered Lexi, the dog preferred gnawing on shoes. Typical, and a dog's way of showing that they love you so much that even the stench of your smelly feet is preferable to a Petco bone. Lexi was a terrier mix, with short fur, pointy ears, and expressive brown eyebrows on a black face. Skye had had Lexi since Skye could remember, and the dog was always with her. Lexi would growl and bark when anyone approached Skye when she was sleeping—which reassured me. Skye had a vulnerability about her, and I didn't like to think of her sleeping in this park each night, even if she *was* eighteen and technically allowed to.

Skye had had a pretty normal life, growing up in a small town in Texas. Her dad worked for the fire department, and she lived with him, her mom, her half sister, and, of course, Lexi. She went to school and earned all As and Bs. She loved watching *Grey's Anatomy* and decided when she was in the eighth grade that she wanted to be a surgeon.

Two years later, everything changed. Skye's dad got sick suddenly and had to be hospitalized. He died of cancer just four days after the family realized something was wrong. Skye was devastated. She'd been close with her dad, but they'd fought right before he got sick because Skye had wanted to go on a date with a girl, and he'd told her she couldn't.

After her dad's death, Skye's grief overwhelmed her. Her grades dropped to Cs and Ds. She was depressed, and within a couple of months she stopped going to school altogether. People in her community tried to help her, but Skye didn't want it—except from Lexi, who she said "knew my grief after my dad died." I was sure she was right. Dogs aren't thoughtful creatures, they're *instinctive* creatures. They rely on their intuition and senses much more than we do, and they pick up on what their owner is feeling or doing. And the more time the animal spends with his owner, the more he absorbs the owner's energy and personality. It's not unlike raising a kid. You don't determine every part of your kid's life, but if you spend a lot of time with them, your influence is going to become a part of them. Lexi was part of Skye, and vice versa. So when Skye said only Lexi knew her pain, I believe Lexi both knew and also probably *felt* it.

After the death of Skye's dad, her mom started to unravel, and things fell apart very quickly. Skye's mom began to drink heavily. She offered alcohol to Skye, who accepted it, and they became daytime drinking buddies. At some point, the two decided they needed a change of scenery. While Skye's half sister stayed in Texas with grandparents, Skye and her mom headed farther west with Lexi.

They drove to San Diego and set up camp in the park by the zoo. Skye loved the beaches and the warm weather of California, but she didn't love being homeless. She felt safe most of the time, she said, but when she got nervous, she would turn to Lexi. Lexi was still helping her with her grief, and now helped her with her anxiety, while still serving watchdog duties at night.

I didn't know this full backstory on the sunny day I met Skye. I examined Lexi, checking her for fleas, peering in her eyes and ears, and feeling her body for any lumps. I could see that Lexi wasn't completely healthy. She hadn't had any vaccinations in five years, she hadn't been spayed—which made her more vulnerable to mammary cancer with each heat cycle—and she had a growth on her lower belly that I tentatively diagnosed as a hernia. As with humans, if a dog's hernia is untreated, it can wrap around an intestine and become life-threatening.

Skye might have been reluctant to trust me with her story, at first, but she did trust me with her dog. She agreed to let me take Lexi to the Beverly Oaks Animal Hospital two hours away. I have a good friend, Dr. Laurel Leach, who owned the practice. A kick-ass vet with purple hair and a huge heart, Dr. Leach was always willing to help me with my street work if she could. She also made me feel inspired to keep going. Like Dr. Pedraza, she reminded me why I got into veterinary medicine in the first place—to heal animals. And she reminded me that people could be awesome, and that they wanted to help. Sometimes you just needed to ask.

Skye, who sometimes appeared distant or checked out, became much more engaged while we examined Lexi. While she was still somewhat shy, she asked specific questions about the procedure, what instruments we would use, and in what order we would approach our work. I recognized the "science spark" in her, because I'd had it myself. I was never a super-studious kid and had to be coerced to read *The Scarlet Letter* and *Great Expectations* (in fact, I may never have read them . . . don't tell my English teachers), but I came alive in science class—and particularly biology. My success in science classes goaded me on, giving me enough motivation to get through the rest of school with at least passing grades so that I could go on to study *just* science. I got there, ultimately, and I wanted Skye to get there, too.

Helping Lexi turned out to be the easy part. Dr. Leach and I put her under anesthesia, spayed her, closed up the hernia, and we even were able to clean her teeth while we were at it. The only complication we encountered was a hole in her abdominal wall—probably caused by a dog bite at some point in her life. We patched that up, too, by pulling over muscle and tissue to close the defect. Not all wounds show on the surface, but that doesn't mean they're not wreaking havoc within—the symbolism of which I hardly need to point out.

Once Lexi recovered, Skye and her mom moved back to Texas, having realized that you can't escape grief by skipping town. My assistant, Genesis, and I stayed in touch with Skye, though, and learned that things only got worse. Skye's mom had gotten hooked on meth while in California, and in Texas she moved in with a drug dealer. Skye started using, too. When Skye's mom found out, she kicked her out—the logic of which baffles me. Skye wasn't on her own, though. She still had Lexi.

Skye didn't give up. She stayed with friends, or with whoever would have her. She worked minimum-wage jobs. She took steps toward getting her GED, though it never quite worked out. Skye was rootless, and a bit lost.

As Skye struggled, Lexi was becoming a problem and biting people. I don't find this all that surprising. Skye was living a life that was chaotic, and probably pretty scary. Skye never voiced that she was angry—she was generally a really accommodating person, the type to shrug her shoulders and say, "It is what it is. What can you do?

So I'll just keep plugging along." It's not hard to imagine that beneath that calm exterior she was angry, nor is it a stretch to imagine her dog picking up on that anger. "Our dog is drawn to wherever our 'charge' is focused," wrote the veteran dog trainer Kevin Behan in *Your Dog Is Your Mirror*, "because it represents an interruption, a disturbance, the holding back of a powerful emotion. If we're compelled by something, so too will be our dog."* Research has shown dogs have an uncanny ability to read human behavior—that they're better at it than chimpanzees. I don't find this surprising, as they've been our companions for so long (whereas not a lot of people have pet chimpanzees!). The point is, all of this evolutionary history was at play for Skye and Lexi, and it meant Skye needed an alternative home for Lexi. Her dad's parents stepped up and took care of the dog—with Skye around as much as she could be.

Then one night, Lexi died in her sleep.

"She'd been through so much with me," Skye told me, her voice despondent. "It was just so hard." Then she changed the subject. She didn't want to talk about Lexi anymore.

* * *

It's not my intent to depress anyone, but the simple truth is that while I haven't met many people on the street as young as Skye, I've met many whose stories follow similar trajectories. Study after study shows that drug and alcohol abuse are multi-generational, and that they are often correlated with experiencing traumas, as Skye did. But studies *also* show that most people—three out of four—who seek

---

* Kevin Behan, *Your Dog Is Your Mirror* (Brilliance Audio, 2022), 15.

help for their addiction recover. That really surprised me—I always figured people with long-standing substance abuse issues didn't have much of a shot. But a 75 percent chance of recovery? I'll take those odds.

It's statistics like these I hold on to when I meet people like Skye, and like Jennifer, who I came across near the San Diego Greyhound station. I'd been driving the streets, and it was clear the police had recently cracked down, which often happened when a group of neighbors complained. Not all shelters accept animals, and not all homeless people are willing to go to one, so more often than not, the camp disperses and its occupants go to their backup locations, the street gets cleaned, and a day or so later everyone's back. We were clearly in one of those cycles, because I didn't find the rows of tents and makeshift awnings on the streets where I usually came across them. But I could always, always count on a row of tents, shopping carts, and sleeping bags near the bus station. Maybe it was because there wasn't residential housing right next to it. Or maybe the police had just ceded the territory.

"I came from a dysfunctional family," Jennifer said. She was Mexican American, and had stringy, long black hair and large brown eyes. She looked to me to be about forty, but life on the street had a way of aging people, and she could actually have been ten years younger. "I did drugs with my mom." She said it in a really matter-of-fact way, and then she began to cry. "That's kind of hard for me to deal with because I . . . resent her for that. All I really wanted was for her to own up to it so we could move on. But when a person can't even do that and doesn't realize there's a problem, you're stuck."

Jennifer had a purebred pug, Solly. "It's overwhelming being on the streets with a puppy," she said. She lived in constant fear of him getting taken—he was her most valuable possession in a monetary sense, but he was also her stability and her joy. She wasn't the only one looking to Solly for some joy. While I examined Solly, we were approached a half dozen times by people who had tents or carts set up near Jennifer, or who were passing through, who wanted to pet his soft puppy folds or be nuzzled by his wet snout.

"There's a lot of people out here who are sick," Jennifer said. "And when I say sick, I mean mentally sick. And they just want to be loved. You know? That's what a lot of people need out here. Just some love."

Though Jennifer's drug use had started with her mom, it worsened when she began to suffer from lupus, a chronic illness that causes inflammation and pain, and has a hereditary piece to it. It can also be brought on by environmental conditions, such as emotional stress and exhaustion. Jennifer had all of these in play—her childhood was full of hardship, and her mom also had lupus. And so the cycle continued. "They put me on medication," Jennifer said of her doctors, "and I liked it. I noticed that when I would take those pills I would be . . . that I felt good. It helped with the pain." And so she found ways to get more pills and became hooked on them. The pills were, of course, opioids.

She was in a relationship with an older man, who she lived with and took care of until he died. The apartment had been registered in his name. "After he died, they evicted me," she said. She was agitated about it and insisted to me that her eviction wasn't legal. I doubted that—if the apartment was registered in his name and paid for with his social security, it made sense the landlords wouldn't allow her to simply stay there. But the bottom line was that Jennifer had nowhere else to go. Between her grief and her opioid use, she couldn't get another plan together, and she and Solly ended up on the streets.

Jennifer hated life on the streets. She just wanted out. She started going to PATH, a nonprofit dedicated to helping the homeless by providing supporting services, including paths to affordable housing. Jennifer goes to the San Diego PATH offices every day, participating in every program she can. "If I leave there, I'll be lost. My goal is to be at least where I was. Where me and Solly were indoors and were safe."

"I just really want to live," she said as I was walking with her and Solly to the public bathroom she uses several times a day. "I don't want to die. Yesterday there was an overdose. There are like five overdoses a day out here. You see death all the time. And I don't want to die. I want to live for my puppy. And for myself."

I was struck not only by how legitimately scared Jennifer was but also by the survival instinct that was so alive in her. She had not given up. She was like a rock climber without a harness, but she had a couple of handholds she was clinging to with all her might. One of those handholds was PATH.

The other was Solly.

It's hard to quantify what these animals do for their owners. Skye did not have a lot of light in her life. Neither did Jennifer. But their dogs connected them to the outside world, and connected them to a love that they were worthy of receiving. As Konrad Lorenz wrote, "It is a fact that one no longer feels alone in the world when there is at least one being who is pleased at one's return home."

After Lexi died, Skye got another dog, a blue heeler named Dakota.

I believe Skye understood she needed a dog to stay alive, for things were still pretty rough. Skye has been addicted to heroin and has overdosed several times. Each time, Dakota was there.

The last time we talked, Skye had been clean and sober for two weeks. She'd been going to Narcotics Anonymous and was participating in a forty-day challenge to ease depression while getting sober. And Dakota stays beside her, always. "When I'm crying or when I really need someone," Skye said, "she'll be right there and let me hug her. She'll sometimes lay her whole body across me. Other times she'll knock my phone out of my hand until I pay attention to her. She helps with my sobriety. If I didn't have her, I don't know where I'd be."

In the movie *Castaway*, once he's returned to civilization, Tom Hanks's character reflects on his years in isolation on the island and how he knew that, though there was little reason to hope, he needed to stay alive anyway and keep breathing. "So that's what I did," the character says. "I stayed alive. I kept breathing."

Dakota is not going to solve Skye's problems, and Solly isn't going to solve Jennifer's. And for that matter, I'm well aware I'm not solving *anyone's* problems. But these animals gave their owners a second chance, and a third chance, and a motivation to just keep breathing, to keep breathing long enough to hopefully, one day, be one of the 75 percent who make it.

Chapter 5

SECOND CHANCES

Looking back on who I was from the ages of seventeen to twenty-three, it's nothing short of a miracle that I stand on the side of the sidewalk I do, holding the stethoscope.

As you know, I was bullied my entire life. But things changed for me in college. For one, I was on the track team, which gave me some status and some confidence. For another, I lifted weights every day after practice, and was amazed at how my body changed. I bulked up—I was no longer the string bean I'd been before puberty. I had a group of great friends in my teammates, and I was still tight with most of the Blues Men. But I also had a lot of anger that I didn't know quite what to do with. I was fit, and strong, and *empowered*. I was like a trained soldier, the tip of a spear—and I wanted to *use* my newfound strength. I had no idea how to manage it, and so I misman-aged it. I'd steal hood ornaments, I'd shoplift, and I'd commit other petty crimes. But mostly, I would fight. I wanted to make good on the promises I'd made to myself as a scrawny kid, that one day when I was big enough, I'd get even.

I carried this quiet rage around with me. I would almost look for people to give me the side-eye, or to make a comment. I had a sensitive detector for being picked on. Once, I came home after a date to the former frat house that I shared with the bunch of guys and found they'd gotten into a big melee with the fraternity across the street. (I think Baron sat it all out from the safety of my room, or Josh's.) My roommates nursed their injuries on the lawn and the porch, and the place looked like the aftermath of a battle. So what did I do? I marched across the street and pounded on the fraternity's door, demanding they let me in so I could mess them all up.

"Go away, Kwane," one of them said. My reputation had apparently preceded me.

I kept pounding, kept threatening them. At one point they opened the door a crack and I could see a half dozen guys waiting on the other side. What did I think was going to happen? Who did I think was going to win this fight? Yeah, it wasn't my brightest moment. It got even crazier, as I decided it would be a good idea to go get a bat, and to come back. By that time, the guys had moved up to their roof, and in my state of mind, I figured, what the hell? And tried to climb up the walls to get there. As I said, not my brightest moment.

But that incident wasn't even the worst of it. One night, I was at a club with some friends, dancing and drinking. Some guy kept bumping into me—and I took it to be intentional. After the third time he bumped me, I squared up to him and said, "What the f**k?" He gave me a look like *what's your problem?* And that's all it took for me to punch him in the face.

Blood flew everywhere from that punch as the guy fell to the ground, screaming and holding his face. My friend Mike was with me and grabbed my arm. "We gotta get out of here, Kwane, now!" So we split.

I might never have known what happened to that guy, except Mike was premed, and dating a woman who was doing her internship at the hospital. Later that night, she and Mike were talking and she said, "We got the craziest case tonight," and she recounted to him that a guy had been punched so hard he had the kind of facial fracture they usually see only with severe-impact car crashes. He would need several reconstructive surgeries to repair the damage.

To say I felt terrible doesn't come close to capturing it. Mike never told his girlfriend it had been me, but he sat me down and said, "Kwane, as you continue to train and get bigger, you could hit someone and kill them. That's what's at stake, man. You'd never mean to. If you struck someone else like you struck this guy, it could kill him, and you would be in prison for the rest of your life."

All I could say was, "You're right." It scared the shit out of me, and I vowed to stop.

Months later, I was out with some friends at Denny's. A guy from across the restaurant stood up and came toward me. He had purplish blue marks on his face—scars. Despite the bruising, and maybe because of it, I recognized him as the guy from the club. He put out his hand and he said, "I just want to apologize for that night." I was speechless. I shook my head, and I shook his hand. I can't remember what words came to me, but it was something like, "No, *I'm* sorry. I can't believe I did that." I still can't get my mind around the grace he showed me, after all I'd put him through. But I'm so, so grateful for it.

If I'd been arrested that night—that would have been it for me. I would have been charged with assault. I would have served time in jail. And then what? Our society isn't one for second chances—that's why I feel so strongly about offering them. That's why I can look at the people I meet and there's just no judgment, zero. Because I am them and they are me. And I think they know that.

* * *

One foggy winter morning when I still worked at the shelter, a stray dog, maybe a year or so old, was brought in. Her fur was a mix of brown and black, and from her coloring and her melty eyes, I guessed she was a pug-Chihuahua mix. What worried me was that she'd bitten the animal control officer who'd captured her. Then she bit my technician. She'd been injured, and was in pain and terrified, which likely explained the biting. But it didn't matter. Between her injuries and her behavior, she was deemed unadoptable. She had just seven days before she'd be put to sleep.

Every time I passed her cage, she'd growl at me. I didn't want to give up on her, though, so every day I would get a little closer to the cage and talk in a slow, sweet voice. Finally, just a day before her time was up, I opened the cage and placed my hand at the edge . . . just waiting (hoping) she would come to it. And she did. She let me stroke the back of her neck, then scratch her belly. Within two minutes she was trying to jump out of the cage into my arms. I cradled her and carried her back to my office. She was starved for attention, but clearly afraid to trust anyone. I removed the euthanasia order, even though she would not be adopted (bite dogs can't be adopted out for liability reasons). She became my little companion.

It took a while for her wounds to heal, by which time everyone at the shelter had become attached to her. We all needed to pull from our networks to find her a home, somehow, since the usual means of adoption wouldn't be possible. I was talking about it with my girl-friend Jamie, and she suggested her mom might be a good match. Debbie was getting on in years, and lived alone, and Jamie thought it would be good for her to have a dog to pull her out of her shell. Debbie wasn't looking for a pet but had a long history of taking in those in need of help—sometimes people, sometimes animals. Maybe, Jamie thought, our matchmaking could help both of them.

Jamie brought her mom by the shelter and introduced them, and it was love at first sight. Debbie adopted the dog, who she named Reesie, on the spot. She took Reesie with her everywhere and became a bit of an amateur photographer, constantly taking pictures of the dog playing or posed just so. We hadn't realized just how lonely Debbie was until we saw the life this dog brought out in her. And we hadn't realized how much capacity for love and affection Reesie had until Debbie brought it out in her.

I think about second chances all the time. And third chances. And fourth chances, because sometimes that's what it takes before animals—and people—find their footing.

* * *

One recent summer day I was spending time at a Tiny Homes complex in LA. The idea with tiny homes is that instead of living in a group shelter, people can have their own small space, and privacy, but with shared resources such as access to social workers and employment programs right outside their door. It can be a great transition to permanent housing. The people who live in Tiny Homes *want* to get back on their feet. But it can take time.

The people who'd signed up to see me that day made up a parade of second chances. There was a man who had just left his abusive partner, because he wanted to do life on his terms, even if it meant homelessness and starting over. Part of starting over meant bringing someone new into his life: a Rottweiler mix he named Pop. There was a tiny woman named Cecilia and her puppy. Cecilia had been in and out of jail, and had also raised her grandchildren and been a manager at a Walmart and a Costco. "I didn't do right by my kids," she said, "but I raised my grandkids well." And then there was Billy, whose tuxedo cat, Smokey, was securely tethered to a leash.

Billy struck me right away as a guy who was trying—and mightily— to get the better of his demons. When we met, he was having trouble moving around because of recent skull fractures. "I don't know how it happened," he said. "I was drinking and I shouldn't have been. They said I was on the freeway when they found me." He acknowledged that he was lucky to be alive, and that he should have been home with Smokey that night, instead of out drinking. Shockingly to me, he said that the doctors had put him on opioids for the pain.

Like so many others I meet, Billy's story started with a tough upbringing—his was in East LA—and a slew of mental health diagnoses. He said he had borderline paranoid personality disorder, PTSD, ADHD, depression, and oppositional defiance disorder. Like his cat, he joked, he wanted to know the *why* behind every little thing he was asked to do, otherwise why would he bother doing it? His mom struggled with an opioid addiction, and Billy was a regular user of meth.

Still, he had skills. He was a stonemason, a trade he'd learned from his grandfather. He worked in the field for five years, and when work dried up, he decided to bet on himself and what *he* wanted to do. And what he wanted was to work with animals. He enrolled in a vet tech program where he did fairly well . . . but, for reasons that were unclear to me, and, I think, to Billy himself, he dropped out just before starting his externship. "I think of going back every day," he said. "I love animals. Animals get me. A lot of people don't get me. But animals get me."

He was homeless for several years, and often would just meander, nomad-like. One night he was in the woods and stumbled on a campsite full of drugged-out people who had a kitten. The group asked if Billy would consider taking the cat. "They said, 'He's too much.' And I thought, 'You know what? I'm too much, too. We'll be out here alone together.'" So he bought the cat and a pack of cigarettes for the bargain price of six dollars. And he and Smokey have been a team ever since. "I'm like a cat," Billy said, pulling a bit on Smokey's leash. "I want affection, but on my terms."

Smokey would sleep for hours on Billy's military-frame backpack, and they've been in some tight spots together. "I've been through a lot," Billy said. "I've had guns in my face in places where you're like, 'What are you gonna do?'" When they were jumped once, Smokey hid, just as he should, Billy said, "because I've got his back. He's my ride-or-die homie."

Smokey is the reason Billy quit meth, he said. "For a while I was almost convinced that I wouldn't survive out there if I stopped doing it. Then I got *him*. And he showed me that I can't have my cake and my cat. I can't have none of that anymore. It's hard to be off meth, but he's worth it. It's one day at a time but everything's for him, everything's for us. We both deserve better."

Billy rarely made eye contact, and his voice was a quiet mumble, but it was clear he had a lot to say as I played with Smokey. "You seem like an intelligent guy who has a trade and can get back on his feet," I said when I finally got a word in. "Can you do that? What's the future?"

"Permanent housing," Billy said, "and then I want to go on with a quiet life. I wanna be retired from the streets."

He also wants a job. "I do better, I *am* better when I work. It gives me purpose. I like to work. I like to learn. I always need a program."

When we said goodbye, I gave Billy my card and told him to let me know when he was ready for work. I thought I could maybe make a call or two to help him get in the door at a vet clinic, but only if he's clean. I haven't heard from him yet. It could be that he found another great opportunity, another job, or that he moved out of the area. It could be that he didn't want to be a vet tech, that that was just something he told me, and it could be that he resented my offer of help.

And it could be that he's not ready for his next chance.

* * *

One thing that Billy had going for him was that if he walked down the street with his cat, no one would be afraid of Smokey. But so many people I meet have the added complication of their animal being intimidating.

It's not exactly news that pit bulls, in particular, have a bad rap. Because of their genetic strength and power, they've sadly been the first choice for criminals who engage in the horrific practice of dog fighting. As such, this breed has carved out its own cultural identity in America and is bought by many who want a "tough" dog. This cycle has continued for decades; now, anytime there's an attack or a bite involving a pit, it grabs headlines. As many in the pet world will tell you, there aren't bad dogs, just bad owners. And unfortunately, pits often get stuck with the worst.

On the flip side, they also match with some of the best. First off, most mixed-breed dogs have some pit bull in them, whether the shelter announces that fact or not. It's much easier to adopt out a dog that you label a "lab mix" than a "pit bull mix." Then there's the fact that because so many pit bulls end up at shelters, where the homeless adopt their dogs, you'll see many pit bulls as street companions. In these relationships, they get to be with their owner 24/7, receive unconditional love, and, as I saw firsthand, excellent training.

I worried, though, when I initially met Loki, a sweet pit-mix puppy who had two problems: one was a problem of perception, as people couldn't see he was a great ball of love; the other was a problem of youthful recklessness that could easily get him hit by a car. His owner, Mario, was a Black man who, of all the people I met on the streets, might have been the most formally polite. He walked stooped over a bit, was missing his two front teeth, and punctuated every sentence with "yes, sir," and "thank you, sir."

I helped Mario and Loki by vaccinating Loki against parvovirus, giving him flea medication, and by setting him up with a friend of mine who was an animal trainer, because I was worried that Loki was too energetic for Mario to handle. The process of all of this took several months, during which I frequently checked in with Mario and got to know him better than most people I encounter. I learned that a lifetime before, he'd been to prison for manslaughter related to gang activity. He hadn't gotten back on his feet since.

I watched Mario work with Loki, teaching him to sit on command, to stay, to come when called, but my mind was elsewhere. I kept imagining how Mario had once been violent—which was almost impossible to fathom. And yet I could. Because most people would look at me and not believe that once, I had been, too.

Chapter 6

THE CALIBRATED
HEART

I've had a lot of moments with younger vets and vet techs where I can tell they're on their last legs in the business. I think I've earned a bit of an armchair psychologist degree for all the advice I've given over the years. Mainly I see that it's so easy for people to get down on themselves when they feel like they're doing something wrong, even if it's something necessary.

I recently had a young vet I work with ask me how I could stay so calm. I'm not built that way—it's definitely something I have to work at. I'm always reminding myself to take a 50,000-year view of whatever it is that's worrying me. Will anyone care in 50,000 years?

I'm not a nihilist—I think what we do and say matters. But the point with the 50,000-year view is that we need to remember events don't matter nearly as much as we think they do. I warn new vets they can get so locked on a moment, thinking they have to be perfect, or hugely successful, and in the end it contributes to pain and anxiety. Keeping that pain and anxiety in check is the only thing that allows us to keep doing our job. Though it took years of experience for me to move through my days with more equanimity, I began that important work during vet school.

Academically, it was much easier for me than undergrad. In part this was because, for the first time in my life, I was motivated to learn every bit of information my teachers could dish out. And in part it was because, toward the end of my undergrad years, I'd gone to the campus learning center to figure out if I had a learning difference. I'd always found it impossible to listen to a professor and take notes at the same time and couldn't figure out *why*. I'd ignored it, mostly, but when I realized the problem could keep me from getting the grades needed for vet school, I decided to get tested.

I found out two things during testing that altered my life going forward. The first was that I did in fact have some learning differences. I was diagnosed with a form of dyslexia and short-term memory processing. The center gave me some tricks to try, and some resources to help, and that was that. My grades improved and I got into vet school by the skin of my teeth. (Truly. I got in off the waitlist and was one of the last two people to be admitted.)

But perhaps the more significant finding came when the neuropsychologist asked if she could run me through a pattern test. The test starts out with simple patterns—two boxes sitting next to each other, then three, and you have to guess what comes next. There are around seventy-five questions and toward the end it gets really difficult—the patterns seem to require complex math to figure out. The doctor told me afterward that she'd only once seen a higher score than mine. "It means that analytically you sit at a genius level," she said, which made me laugh, because I'd always been a middling-to-average student. But she went on to explain that while we typically think of intuition as this nebulous feeling, it's actually a collection of information and experience that become data points. Your mind processes all of this, she said, and spits out to do this or do that, to "choose a or choose b."

I'd always heard the cliché "trust your intuition," but what this test taught me was that my intuition wasn't a weird voice, it was my brain working hard on my behalf, recognizing patterns and letting them inform my next move. "You scored so well on this test," she said, "that it's almost like you have a crystal ball." She didn't use these words, but she essentially told me to trust my inner fortune-teller. (Years later I'd listen to Malcolm Gladwell's book *Blink*, on the same subject, and recognize that this doctor was ahead of her time.)

Since that conversation at the learning center, I've let my intuition be my ultimate guide in life. To this day if I get a feeling to stop the car when I see someone at the side of the road with a dog, I'm more likely to do it than think about all the reasons I shouldn't.

I didn't think it would come off well to tell my new vet school classmates that I had a fortune-teller in my head, so I mostly kept it to myself. But I felt a change in me, a newfound confidence.

My class was composed of 126 students, and we stayed close throughout the four years of vet school. I'd always been around smart people—the Blues Men were some of the most intelligent kids in high school—but my vet school classmates weren't just smart; they were driven, ambitious, and passionate about animals. The friendships I made during vet school made the first two years much more exciting than they should have been—because far from treating actual animals, we mostly spent our time sitting in lecture halls and taking tests.

Finally in junior year, we got to spend half the day in the veterinary teaching hospital, shadowing senior students. My first day at the hospital, I put on my blue smock for the first time. It still had the pressed line in it, the sharp fabric smell. I zipped it up, put my pens in my pocket, and looked at myself for a long time in the mirror, thinking, *It's happening.*

The work itself wasn't that glamorous. We spent our time restraining animals and running errands. But we got to see all of the different disciplines, from radiology to triage to surgery, and I was exhilarated. I don't drink caffeine but every day I'd go to school like I'd slammed a Red Bull, or like I was a six-year-old headed to Disneyland.

I lost Baron during those years, completely unexpectedly. I came home from class one day and he was lying down, just *gone.* He'd been eating and drinking normally, and I'd even taken him on a walk that morning and nothing had seemed amiss. I didn't even feel sad at first, I was just shocked. How had this happened? *Why* had this happened? The scientist in me kicked in, and I brought Baron's body into the teaching hospital. I thought maybe we could do a postmortem exam, that I could be present for it and help sort out the mystery. Then, maybe, I could make sense of the loss.

As it happened, I couldn't participate. My emotions kicked in and I recognized there was no way I could be a part of a postmortem on my own dog, my *first* dog. I sat outside the hospital and processed my grief instead. A cause of death was never discovered anyway, and as much as I might have wanted to hide behind science, sometimes you just have to accept that there are no explanations—death happens, and grief is the only thing that's necessary.

* * *

I knew even then that my interest was in small animals, that I wanted to practice what's called "companion animal medicine." I didn't want to spend time studying horses and cows. But all vet students had to take rigorous, comprehensive board exams in order to practice veterinary medicine, where we were expected to carry the knowledge on a dozen species, their physiology and anatomy, from snakes to dolphins to cows.

That's why I took a bovine class that required us to head out to a farm and check to see if dairy cows were pregnant. Fourteen of us lined up behind fourteen cows, who were happily eating in their stalls. We each put on a plastic glove that ran up to our shoulder, and slapped goo all over it. The next step was to insert our hand through the cow's rectum, move it up to about our elbow length, and palpate for a fetus. We'd gone through the steps in class, now it was time to actually *do* it.

I stood next to one of my close friends, Wade, who had ranch hand experience. I watched him, but acted like I wasn't, because I didn't want to seem totally incompetent. When I put my hand in, I could only push it in up to my forearm. It's like I'd hit a cul de sac that wasn't supposed to be there. Worse yet, my cow was vocalizing— the only one out of the fourteen to do so.

"Hey, Wade," I said, "I think I'm doing something wrong." I couldn't fake it anymore. Everyone knew something was up, anyway, since my cow had a lot to say.

Wade looked over and smiled. "You've got your hand in her vagina, not her ass."

James Herriott I was not.

I was embarrassed, but overall vet school makes you feel it's safe to "practice." You're at a veterinary *teaching* hospital, after all, and when the animal owners come in for treatment, they know it. There are always competent people around who will help you out if you're about to screw up. We were instructed time and time again, "You're going to make mistakes. Learn from them, then move on." They also taught us about compassion fatigue, but I didn't remember a word of it. One of the school's main mantras was "watch one, do one, teach one," but while that might work for placing a catheter, you can't practice the heartache of losing animals.

The most valuable lessons I learned, though, were from an externship I did in Milwaukee, Wisconsin, between my junior and senior years. I assisted a veterinarian, Dr. Jacques Thebert, who ran a small practice he'd inherited from his dad. I was twenty-five, he was in his late thirties, and we had a lot in common. He'd take me out for beers after work (Milwaukee met its reputation as a beer-drinking culture), and we'd talk about sports and all the things I shouldn't worry about. In fact, his most frequent admonition was "don't worry about that."

Jacques practiced a brand of old-school medicine he'd learned from his father. He said, "Look, in vet school they're going to teach you about pheochromocytoma. It's an adrenal disease. It comes with a very puzzling pathophysiology, and there's a lot to it."

I nodded, because in my junior year, we'd spent an exhaustive amount of time talking about exactly this disease.

"The thing is," Jacques said, "you might see one or two cases of it in your career. And it drives me crazy because I get these externs in and they can't identify an ear mite in a cat because they're too busy looking for a pheochromocytoma. Common things are common. Know the stuff you need to know daily, and you can always look the rest up."

Jacques also told me about how I'd feel when I lost my first patient. "You'll wonder if you've done everything you could. And then you'll have to go into the next room and treat another animal. Vet school can't teach you to compartmentalize—only experience can. You might have a pet die in triage—say a dog rolls in on a gurney and it's just like in a movie. The owners are shouting out what happened, what went wrong, and you'll try to resuscitate the dog and it will die. Then you have to tell the owner, and then move on to your next case or patient, who has no idea what's just happened. That's the tough part of being a medical practitioner, Kwane," he said.

"There was a life that ended," he went on, "and you were the man on the job. But this is what we do. You're tasked with a giant responsibility as a vet, but you're not here by mistake. You've earned your spot and you're going to get through it. You have the coping skills—you've trained for this, and you're going to be okay. Just don't worry too much."

* * *

Jacques was a key force in training me to keep my cool, and my dad was another. Because, of all the things Jacques understood about being a white veterinarian in Milwaukee, he didn't know much about being a Black man in America. And no one but my dad could teach me about that.

I continued my workout regimen in vet school, and my vet school buddy Rick and I would go to a gym three or four times a week. We were on the bench press one day, alternating spotting each other, when out of nowhere, these two guys walked up to us. One guy said, "I've got a joke for you." I'd seen him around the gym but didn't know him, so it seemed strange. He was clearly talking to me, not Rick. But Rick—a white guy from a Kentucky farm—got off the bench, his attention heightened.

This guy said, "Why do Black guys cry after sex?" I looked at Rick, who seemed as confused as I was. The guy said, "It's a reaction from the mace." Then he and his friend laughed and walked away.

My reflex was a bit of a laugh, but I was also frozen in place. I looked at Rick and said, "Wait a minute, what does that mean?"

Rick looked uncomfortable, then said, "I don't think it's good."

"Is he trying to say that a Black guy must be trying to rape a woman?"

"I don't know, man," Rick said. "But yeah, I think so."

I got on the bench and started to do my set, then stopped. *What the hell?* I racked the weights and walked over to the guy, Rick close behind me.

"Hey," I said. "I don't get the punch line of your joke."

"You know what it means," he said.

"No," I said, "I don't."

"You know exactly what it means, coon."

Rick sprung into action, pulling me away and yelling, "You're an asshole!" to the guy.

I broke free of Rick, grabbed the offender, and turned him around to face me. I had his shirt clenched with one fist and was rearing back to hit him with the other.

At that point the gym manager rushed over. "I don't know what's going on here," he said. "But knock it off or take it outside."

I released the guy and said, "You go ahead and wrap up your workout. I'm going to be waiting right outside the door for you."

Rick spent the next ten minutes trying to talk me down, but he waited with me outside. "The guy's a racist asshole, Kwane. Just forget it."

I couldn't help myself from asking something I'd wanted to ask since the moment I met Rick. Like I said, he was from Kentucky, and had been in an all-white fraternity in college. I didn't need to ask to know I was his first Black friend. But there was one thing I didn't know. "Have you ever said anything like that?"

"You know me, Kwane. I haven't. I wouldn't."

I believed him, but he still couldn't talk me out of staying and waiting for the guy. In a few minutes a truck full of rednecks dramatically screeched to a stop next to me and Rick. *Ha, so he'd called on reinforcements.* It was only then that the offender walked out of the gym.

The truck doors opened and six guys surrounded me and Rick. "Hey," one said, "we hear you're trying to cause trouble with our friend."

"Your friend is trying to cause problems with *me*," I said.

"Well," said another, "looks like you'll have to deal with all of us."

"I guess I will."

I'll never forget Rick's loyalty that day, that he pulled his shoulders back and said, "Okay. I guess we're going to do this."

I looked straight at the biggest guy and said, "Am I going to take care of you first, or the scared people behind you?" Before he could answer, I shoved him. As he stumbled, the manager came out and shouted, "We're calling the cops!"

It was enough to disperse the tension, and our crowd. Had that manager not come out, it's likely Rick and I could have been seriously hurt. I was big—bigger than I'd ever been—but we were also outnumbered.

Nothing happened, and no one got hurt, but it was one of the hardest days of my vet school years. I might have been in my twenties, and a big guy in a professional school, but I called my dad crying that night. It was something I'd never done before. And my dad got choked up too, which I'd only rarely seen from him. He's not completely emotionally cut off, but he has a military bearing. My dad grew up in the Deep South in the 1950s and '60s—he's seen more racism in his life than I can possibly imagine—but he'd never become emotional when talking to us about it. It was easier, I think, for him to endure racism than to have his son experience it.

Still, his emotion did not override his cool head. I wanted him to agree with me that those guys at the gym were evil, but he wouldn't. "These people don't know what they're doing, they don't know what they're saying, Kwane. And you can beat them down, but in the long run it doesn't make you feel any better, son. Trust me."

He was right to preach calm justice, I guess, because the next day, the gym manager reached out to me and said, "We revoked that guy's membership. You won't see him again." I was gratified. He didn't even ask me a single question about why I'd reacted as I had.

A month or two later, I saw the offending guy at the gym again. He came straight over to me and said, "What I did that day was wrong, and I wanted to come here and apologize. I'm sorry." He held out his hand. I stood there, contemplating whether to shake it or hit him.

Before I could think too much, I shook his hand.

I don't know why. Maybe it was my dad in my head. Maybe it was that guy at Denny's who had shown me grace after I'd hurt him badly. Maybe it was my inner fortune-teller, guiding me to a response based on infinite data that I couldn't break down, exactly, but that I could feel.

* * *

"Dr. Kwane!" Diana greeted me with a big hug, and I was struck by just how tiny she was—much smaller than the huge husky she'd just been playing tug-of-war with. I was also struck by the fact that she was still here, at the Stanislaus County Animal Shelter. I'd come back for a visit several years after I'd left, just to say hi to some old friends and check out how things were going. Happily, things were going well, and the shelter's live release rate (the percentage of animals who were successfully adopted) was creeping ever upward. I don't know why it surprised me that Diana was still there—she had always been our most committed volunteer. But still—it had been ten years since she'd first come in. Who volunteers somewhere six days a week, seven or eight hours a day, for *ten years*?

Well, Diana does.

Diana was probably in her late fifties when she first came to the shelter looking for a way to help out. She was retired, an empty nester, and looking for a community of like-minded animal lovers and a way to fill her days. Her job at the shelter was not glamorous. She primarily cleaned kennels and scooped poop. She made sure the dogs got exercise, in 90-degree weather under the blaring sun. But she also cuddled kittens and got to know the personalities of each and every dog. When someone came into the shelter looking to adopt an animal, Diana was the best salesperson, because she knew them all. No one who came in was going to leave without the right animal for them. In that way, she was like the mythical bookseller who sizes up a customer, disappears into the stacks, and comes back with exactly the right book for them.

"How have you been?" I asked her.

"Good, good. Always good."

"Do you have a dog right now?" I asked.

"Yes," she said. "All of these are my dogs."

So that was a no.

You'd think, if anyone should have an animal of their own, it was Diana. And she *had* had a dog—two, in fact. They were tiny, six-week-old mixed-breed puppies when they came into the shelter—much too young to survive there, because they weren't yet eligible for critical vaccinations. And as much as we tried to keep dogs separated and healthy, there was just too much sickness going around the shelter at that time for a little puppy's immune system. They needed to be fostered, and Dorothy, the shelter supervisor at that time, asked Diana if she would do it.

"Oh, please don't do this to me," Diana had said. She knew how hard it would be to foster them, to grow attached, and then to see them go to a different family. But she told Dorothy she'd think about it, because she saw how scared, and how tiny, they were. "I'll give you an answer by the end of the day," she told Dorothy. And, just as I had with Sushi, she caved.

She brought those puppies home and gave them all of her love and care until they were old enough to be adopted out. But by then, of course, they were Diana's dogs. They weren't going anywhere. The shelter offered to spay and neuter them for free, given Diana's commitment and the sweat equity she'd put in over the years, but Diana—who surely lived on a fixed income—insisted on paying. It's a gesture that impresses me every time I think of it.

Unfortunately, three years later, both dogs got very sick with cancer, and died within six months of each other. Diana was devastated. Seven years after their deaths, she was still not willing to bring a pet home. She had her pets—they just didn't live with her.

I've worked with a lot of pet lovers like Diana over the years, people who work in the space of animal welfare because they see it as a calling. It's a field that offers so much joy and reward; you get the immediate gratification of a wagging tail or a purr that tells you these animals love you back, and that they need you. I've encountered some pretty inspiring pet lovers. I've met people who make it a habit to buy extra dog food every time they go to the store, to donate to homeless pets. I met veterinary students who will volunteer their scarce time to help animals of the homeless, and I've met people who are devoted to bringing spay-and-neuter clinics to developing countries.

What I've noticed over the years is that everyone has their own method for guarding their heart—or, like Diana, they figure it out as they go. It takes calibration to love and to give and, ultimately, to lose—as most pet lovers survive their pets. Too much heart and the veterinarian, vet tech, pet lover, or advocate will burn out. Too little heart and they wouldn't be there in the first place, or they wouldn't be trusted to do right by the animals in their care. But calibration is not easy. And the hard truth is that not everyone can do it and some have to walk away to preserve their mental health. There's no shame in that.

The closest relationships I've had with other animal lovers are with vet techs. There's a sometimes weird dynamic between vet techs and veterinarians, though. I imagine it's similar to what nurses and doctors experience in a hospital setting. The techs are deferential to the vets, who they technically work for. And yet we're in the trenches *together*, and it's the techs who know everything that's going on. They have their eyes on both the big picture and the day-to-day minutiae. They aren't paid well, and yet they're the ones drawing blood, the first ones to talk to the animal owners, and, in the shelter, the ones euthanizing most of the animals—an impossibly difficult task, but one that brings with it a very level sensibility. Vet techs know the stakes of the profession intimately. A gifted vet tech will have a mix of people skills, project management proficiency, technical know-how, and a big heart, carefully calibrated. It takes a special kind of person.

At the Stanislaus County Animal Shelter, I would not have lasted a day were it not for my right hand, Paisley. Because, added to the list of skills above, she also had a great sense of humor, and we had a light rapport that kept us going when things felt very dark. I saw her and my other tech, Bette, more than I saw my family. There were days when the shelter felt like a wartime environment, with one crisis after another, and our bonds were forged on these days. On one occasion, we were faced with putting down a litter of Doberman puppies who were infected with parvovirus. We had one day to find alternate placement for them, because if they stayed in the shelter, we risked infecting all the other animals. It was a race against the clock, and the odds for success were stacked well against us, but we did it— we saved every pup that day. On another day, the floor collapsed at our adoption center—four mobile homes put together—which was occupied by some seventy animals. We did endless neuters in a converted trailer we dubbed the "Neuter Scooter." Put simply, it was a lot to deal with. Some days felt impossibly dark. Bette, Paisley, and I could easily have spiraled downward together. But Paisley would never have let that happen.

Paisley was tough as nails, and I never, ever saw her cry. She had a squeaky voice and a short stature, but she had an air of authority that made people pay attention, like a sergeant. She was no-nonsense, and she didn't suffer fools lightly. In a story that became legendary around the shelter, once a man and his son came in with a black-and-white puppy whose ears were badly infected. The man had foolishly tried to crop them for aesthetic reasons (which used to be popular with some breeds). He hadn't done a good job, and the act had undoubtedly been painful for the dog. Paisley was working the desk. "I heard you have a vet here," the man said. "Can you guys fix his ears for free?" Paisley explained that as a shelter, we didn't do work like that, and that he'd have to go to a regular vet and pay their fee. The man looked downhearted, so Paisley said, "I'll tell you what I'll do. I'll pay to get that dog's ears fixed. But first I get to cut yours."

Yeah, that was Paisley in a nutshell. She'd hardened against people, but never, *ever* against animals.

It took a while for me to piece together Paisley's story—we were usually too busy doing triage, so while we had many moments of quick banter, we didn't have a lot of time to really talk. But over the years as I learned more about her, it fell into place for me why she was so good at her job.

Paisley had an upbringing that was rough around the edges. She actually had a lot in common with some of the people I met on the streets, in that her mom was an addict. Through a chaotic childhood, Paisley took comfort in animals, and there were *always* animals around the house—dogs and cats of all different sizes and breeds. But then Paisley's mom would decide she'd had enough and would get rid of them. Paisley never knew where they went, and never had a chance to say goodbye. But it didn't affect her ability to get attached to them. The family would get a new crop of animals, and those would again become Paisley's main source of comfort.

Paisley had a tough relationship with her mom, needless to say, and that transferred to her relationships with men, too. "I was always in abusive relationships," she told me once. She had a son from one of these relationships, who she swore to always protect. Her main focus was supporting her boy. She got a cosmetology license after high school and spent her days doing hair. She and her boyfriend also adopted a red pit bull, Karl, who she rescued from a backyard breeder.

"I remember one day," she said, "I was standing while doing this guy's hair, and he was looking at all the pictures I had up of Karl and other animals I'd had. The guy said, 'Why are you doing hair? You obviously love animals.'" Something clicked for Paisley in this moment. She'd been so preoccupied by how to make enough to support herself and her son that she hadn't even thought about combining her need to make a living with her love for animals. This brief conversation inspired her to look into career paths, and when she saw a living wage could be made as a tech, she enrolled in a program to get her associate degree.

One night during this career shift, things got particularly bad with Paisley's boyfriend, and she and her son took off. They had to leave Karl behind, and before Paisley could retrieve him, tragedy struck. A firework landed on the roof of the boyfriend's house and it caught fire—the police and fire department showed up, and in the ensuing chaos, Karl was killed.

"He was killed on October third," Paisley said as if it had just happened, though it was years before, "and I started my job at the shelter on October fifteenth."

It was not a soft landing—the shelter didn't have a regular veterinarian when Paisley arrived a few years before me, so Paisley would jump from one boss to another all the time. One of her first responsibilities was euthanizing dogs—not exactly the cushiest assignment. The procedure was done in a cold room with green walls and a concrete floor. One of Paisley's colleagues told her that in years prior, it had served as a gas chamber for dogs—the dogs would be left in kennels in the room, and the shelter employee would hit a button when they left the room that would activate gas cylinders. It was a horrible practice, and while euthanasia was done more humanely—by injection—by the time Paisley arrived on the scene, the room felt cold, almost haunted. On one of her first days, Paisley had to euthanize a hundred dogs—

all puppies—in that room. "There was nothing wrong with them," she said. "It was just for space. This was before I had any kind of control. I was brand new. I just did what I was told. That was before I knew what I could do."

It took her six months to realize that she was good at what she did, and that she had a way of talking to those she worked with that gave her a kind of authority—she was a leader. "I realized I had some influence, and that I could make life a lot better for the animals if I stayed." Instead of doing the euthanasia on the cold concrete floor, for instance, she brought comforters in. She brought dog treats in. She didn't muzzle the dogs if she could help it, so they were more relaxed. "If they were terrified," she said, "I would sedate them before I did it." She couldn't prevent the need for euthanizing the animals, but she brought humanity to the act—and that is everything. Knowing that she was making a difference to these animals—even if it was small, even if it was just in the last moments of their lives—gave her the sense of purpose she needed to stay.

In fact, Paisley never wanted to miss work, because if she did, we wouldn't be able to do as many spay/neuters. Since we had a limited number of days we could keep the animals before euthanizing them, and because they had to be neutered or spayed before they were deemed adoptable, Paisley knew that if she took a day off work, it would mean the clock would run out on more animals.

If Paisley had to leave the shelter to grab lunch or do an errand, she would never wear her scrubs that identified where she worked. On more than a few occasions, when people found out what she did, they yelled "animal killer!" at her. This kind of treatment happens all the time to people who work at shelters. I've been accused of the same, called a "killer bastard," as if I had a choice. And let me tell you, it takes a toll.

The combination of it all—the death, the abuse by ignorant members of the public—it all chips away at you. When I think back to those days at the shelter, for so many of us, our personal lives were falling apart. I've long theorized that there was a causal effect. Work just took everything out of us, so that we didn't have anything left for the people we loved . . . and they knew it.

Paisley once told me, "Shelter work either makes you more compassionate, or it makes you not. For me, I never hardened toward animals. I never lost my drive to help them. . . . When those animals came into the shelter, they were mine. I treated them like they were my own." She always had an edge toward people—especially the ones who deserved her edge—but was just like a child with the animals. She was consistent, too, in the way she would talk to them, pet them, treat them with respect, regardless of the breed, regardless of whether they were a beautiful purebred or a mutt with a nasty eye infection.

It was a lesson for me to watch Paisley. To see someone be able to work so consistently under duress, and still be able to maintain her composure. If she ever came in distraught, it was because of something that happened with her son or her boyfriend. But the stuff that would crush most people? Not Paisley. She worked at that shelter for more than ten years. That's a lifetime and a half for someone in shelter medicine.

It wasn't a surprise to me that when Paisley did finally leave the shelter, it wasn't because of the animals, but because of a personnel issue. She disagreed with how animals were being handled and resigned in protest. Even in her departure, she was protecting them. Now she's in charge of a spay-and-neuter clinic right next door. She is still, and forever will be, keeping unwanted animals from a hard fate.

"Someone had to do it," she told me recently of her time at the shelter. "I would rather do it than let someone who could care less about them do it. I wanted to do more than just bitch about all the unloved animals in the world.

"I did it for as long as I could stand it."

* * *

When I'd been doing my street work for a few years, I recognized that I could be much more effective, and reach more people, if I had some help. I needed experienced hands to hold the animals as I vaccinated them, and to draw blood for tests while I talked to the owners about the reason for those tests. I started asking around, and Genesis's name came to the top of the list.

Ever since Genesis was a kid, she'd been obsessed with helping animals. She had her own farm in the backyard of the family's house, with chickens, rabbits, mice, and a rat. She regularly put out cardboard boxes lined with blankets so that stray cats would have somewhere warm to spend the night. Genesis was only eight at the time, but recognized that a stray cat was pregnant, so upgraded the expectant mama to the small trailer that was parked in the backyard. Her mom went in one day and screamed, thinking it had been infested with mice. But Genesis was joyful and squealed, "She had her kitties!" Genesis took care of those babies and found homes for all of them. When she visited her uncle's farm in Rosarito, Mexico, she would beg her dad to buy her tacos, then feed all the meat to the area dogs.

Genesis was always interested in science, and when she got older her dad encouraged her to pursue nursing school. While she studied nursing, she got a part-time job as a receptionist at an animal hospital, and immediately began grilling all the veterinarians and techs about what they were doing and why. The more she investigated animal science, the more she was hooked; it brought the animal-loving girl she had always been to the forefront of her life.

Two crucial things happened to her while she was working as a technician at the very hospital where she'd been a receptionist. First, she developed a bond with a Pekingese client, Snuggles, who came in frequently because of his seizures. Snuggles's owner, an older gentleman, could see right away that Snuggles and Genesis had a special connection. So could everyone else at the hospital—they knew not to interfere when Snuggles came in, because Genesis would take care of him. When Snuggles's owner became terminally ill with cancer, he gave Snuggles to Genesis. "He said we belonged together," she said.

The second thing that happened was that one day at the hospital, she was taking care of a German shepherd who'd been badly neglected by his owner. He'd been left much too long on his own, and had painful sores on his hips. Genesis got down on the floor with him and spooned him during her breaks and every quiet moment she could find. She told him that she loved him and that he was a good dog. One of her colleagues asked her what she was doing, and she said, "I'm showing him what love is, because he doesn't know what that feels like." The dog passed away the next day, but the story of Genesis spooning this German shepherd spread far and wide, and she was nominated for the Hero Veterinary Nurse Award. While she didn't win, I met her at the awards gala, and then her name came up again when I was asking a veterinarian friend of mine who she would recommend as an assistant. "She's perfect," my friend said. "She already goes around and gives food and toys to animals on the streets. Talk to her."

So I did, and that was that.

True to her reputation, when I started working with Genesis I saw that her animal love was truly next-level. When we were at lunch one day, she started talking to the pigeons who were scavenging for food. "Hey there, baby," she called in a singsongy voice, "you hungry?" She rescued a butterfly at a concert in Anaheim, took it home, and nursed it back to health. It would perch on her shoulder when she walked outside, until it was strong enough to fly away. One winter she was visiting Big Bear Lake, in the Sierra Nevada, and saw a duck caught on a fishing line a ways out in the water. She couldn't find a canoe, so she went out to free it in her damn jeans. She took the duck to the humane society, and when the vets there couldn't save it, she was devastated.

Animals didn't always return her tenderness. She has a finger joint that's all messed up from a cat bite, and that will undoubtedly give her trouble as her bones age. She's been bitten on her hand and on her face—both by dogs. She's been kicked by a donkey. Genesis and I tease about all of her bites. She has pointed out on more than one occasion that since a tech can get written up for reporting a bite, techs keep them quiet. A part of the industry, she said, and sighed. My view is that she probably wasn't careful enough, to have gotten so many injuries. That her heart was so big, she just couldn't help herself from getting close to animals with which she probably should have exercised caution.

I knew vet techs took the worst of it—both in terms of pain and in blame. It's true that it's a black mark on a tech's record if they get bitten. But it's also a black mark if the doctor gets bitten. When I'm treating an animal, I'm focusing on palpating its stomach, or checking its ears. I'm not looking at behavior because that's the tech's job. If a tech gets distracted and misses an animal's increased agitation, and that agitation leads to the animal biting the doctor, they lose. If the animal bites the tech, they lose then, too. They could formally report the bite, but then they're done for the day, because they have to go to the hospital and get checked out for liability purposes. So it turns into a natural response for them to say, "I'm good, I'm good," to bandage their injuries and move on. They're tough—and Genesis is one of the toughest.

One of the first things Genesis told me about herself was that Snuggles had saved her life. She was living alone at the time, and was having a lot of family problems. Work was particularly tough—the long hours, and also just the emotional nature of it. "I felt like I wasn't doing enough. I didn't feel satisfied. I didn't think I was doing enough for the animals, and felt like I had no purpose. I remember sitting on my bedroom floor and staring at myself in the mirror and thinking, *I'm done, this is it*. Something I would say to myself a lot was *When God made me He wasted a human*. I hate saying that. I was almost to the bottom of a bottle of Johnnie Walker, and I didn't want to be alive anymore."

At this low point she stared at Snuggles and said, "I love you, buddy." He walked over to her with his funny walk and very deliberately pushed the bottle of Johnnie Walker over. "I just snapped out of it when he did that," she said, "and I thought, *What the fuck are you doing?*" She wasn't alone. She had Snuggles, and she couldn't leave him.

After that day, Genesis had a devotion to Snuggles that looked just like the connection I see on the streets between animals and their pets. It's a connection borne of desperation, a connection of codependency, but the good kind. The kind that saves lives.

When Snuggles died years later, Genesis was in a better place in her life—a place where Snuggles was no longer the only thing keeping her from finishing the job she'd started with the Johnnie Walker. But her devotion to that dog was so absolute that she didn't know how she would ever get another one. "I know this sounds weird to other people, but Snuggles was my best friend. And I know he's not with us, but I don't want him to feel like I'm replacing him." Genesis did consider other dogs occasionally, but it never worked out. Finally, six years after she lost Snuggles, Genesis adopted a Chihuahua-terrier mix named Pickles.

That Genesis had such a huge heart for animals was an absolute asset for my street work. I knew that the people we offered to help would see it right away. She would go in, straight for the animal, and as people saw her do that, they recognized a kindred spirit and trusted her. It was also helpful that Genesis's family is from Mexico, and that she speaks fluent Spanish, which I don't. As we do our work in Southern California, her language skills often made all the difference in making someone feel comfortable and that they could trust us.

As she would chat with our street clients, they were instantly able to see an animal lover, someone who shared at least some common background with them, and lest they feel intimidated by Genesis's air of glamour (she trains for bikini competitions in her spare time), she has a very distinctive snort when she laughs, which is just dorky enough to disarm them.

I was so grateful to have Genesis along while I did my street work. And as I'd expected, we were much more efficient, as simple procedures that had been awkward before were a piece of cake with Genesis holding the animal. She was great at blood draws, and for whatever reason, she didn't mind expressing dogs' anal glands— never my favorite task. And like with Paisley, we also had a nice, teasing rapport, which kept things light during inevitably tense and dark moments.

While a lot of animal people will sometimes show a hardness when it comes to people, as Paisley did, that wasn't the case with Genesis. She would have taken every single person we met home with her to take care of them if she could. In fact, she kept in close touch with Skye, from an earlier chapter—and offered on more than one occasion to have Skye live with her. Whereas I was always careful about entanglement, and felt I needed to have a clear divide between my street work and the rest of my life in order to preserve my sanity, Genesis didn't have any of that. I can't count the number of times I'd turn to Genesis after talking to someone we met on the street, and find her wiping her eyes.

In our two-person street team, Genesis and I complement each other. She's the heart, and I'm the brains. We both have a part of each, obviously. I wouldn't be good at what I do if I was completely cold and cut off; and if she was all heart, she wouldn't be nearly as helpful. But sometimes I suspect we lean too much on the other to play our designated roles. Genesis can give in to her overwhelming compassion sometimes because she knows I'll be steady. And I can push away the sadness I feel on the harder days we have because I know someone else is there to absorb it all.

Still, I've said to Genesis many times that if she keeps going this way, if she keeps giving all of herself with every interaction, she's not going to last in this business. She already has insomnia. She carries every lost animal or lost human we encounter with her, and that's too much for anyone to hold. And I really want Genesis with me for the long haul.

There was one day in San Francisco when I thought Genesis might be done for good. We met a man named Carl on the streets who looked like a slightly younger, slightly heavier version of Anthony Hopkins. Carl had two dogs, Cephas and a brand-new puppy, Matthew. "They keep me going," he told us, and though we'd barely started talking, he was crying. "They make me get up and move, and pack my stuff. 'Cause I know that I have to take care of them. This is my family. They love me."

It was hard to see Carl's raw vulnerability. He'd done an amazing job caring for his dogs—they were healthy and up to date on their vaccinations. But San Francisco also gets cold, and he struggled to keep them warm enough. This really got to Genesis. "You know how people will say, 'Oh, it's just a dog'?" she told me after we said good-bye to Carl. "But to me, dogs aren't just dogs. Animals aren't just animals. I think what got to me was that his dog Matthew looked like Pickles and I put myself in his shoes. Carl said that his dogs are what keep him going. Pickles was why I kept going, too. How would I do it if I were out here with Pickles and it was cold? Or I didn't have food for her? How would I do that?"

I didn't have a comforting answer for Genesis, and probably spent a minute just unhelpfully staring. I tried to channel Jacques, and knew what he would say: "Don't worry about it." Most of the things we worry about never come to pass, he'd said. And if they did—if Genesis did find herself out in the cold with Pickles—she would do what Carl was doing: whatever it took to keep her animal and herself warm until she could get back on her feet again. What I wanted to say, but didn't in that moment, was that she needed a more calibrated heart. I couldn't tell her that, though, just as they couldn't teach it in vet school. It's something you learn through years of hard experience.

Genesis doesn't work for Street Vet full-time. She's also not a vet tech anymore. But she's never far from animals. She spends her days working for a pet insurance company, where I can only imagine what a great salesperson she is for the need to protect your animals by insuring them. She's a natural evangelist, because she remembers countless times of having to place a bill in front of an owner for their animal's care that they wouldn't be able to pay. The look on the owner's face when they didn't have insurance was heartbreaking, and she goes around to educate people so that no one is ever faced with making such a difficult choice, and vets aren't put in the situation where they have to put down an animal that is loved and wanted but whose care is prohibitively expensive.

I've been in that situation too many times. Most veterinarians have. It's one of the reasons, I believe, that there is such a high suicide rate for those who work in veterinary care—one in six veterinary professionals consider suicide at some point in their career, which is much higher than in other professions.

The suicide rate of veterinary professionals is an issue that's finally getting some attention in the industry. A nonprofit called NOMV, or Not One More Vet, is leading the charge. Started by a woman whose best friend, a veterinarian, committed suicide, it aims to bring some of the financial and mental health challenges of vet care to the surface. As its website explains, "Not Good Enough" is the mantra of so many people who work in vet care. "The words that flash through your mind after you are unable to save an animal. And whether the problem was medical, financial, or something else . . . the message is the same. I've failed. And when you carry this weight, the other stressors of working in a veterinary practice can feel unbearable. The bright, impassioned idealism to be the protector and savior of animals turns to ash, and depression begins to take over your life. You didn't fail. This is not the life we want for you. And there is hope."

Because of the increased attention to mental health in the field, vet schools and vet tech schools are taking more seriously that they need to train students about burnout and compassion fatigue, just as doctors and nurses are trained. And, by the way, burnout and compassion fatigue are very different. Heidi Shaw runs a mental health program for a chain of vet clinics, and says people get the two confused all the time. Burnout is often caused by working too much and with too few resources. When a place is understaffed, or underfunded, and people don't have the equipment or space to do their job well, burnout is likely. Burnout comes on slowly, and rarely catches anyone completely by surprise—it's also prevalent in any industry when there's too much work and too few people and resources to do it. Compassion fatigue comes on much more quickly. You can have very little to do in a day and still experience compassion fatigue, which is when you are taking in the strong emotions of someone else, like breathing secondhand smoke. Experiencing either, and not doing something about it, is really detrimental to mental health.

Burnout isn't exactly easy to address, but at least it's more tactical. It involves changing systems or changing expectations of just how much work can actually be done by one person. Compassion fatigue is much harder to recognize and support. Everyone has to find their own way through compassion fatigue, because there's not a one-size-fits-all answer. And it's not something that goes away so much as it's something to be managed. Heidi, for instance, grew up working at her aunt and uncle's cattle ranch in Nebraska. Part of her daily tasks involved getting rid of animals that had died in the night, and fattening up the ones who survived so they could be taken to slaughter. Her aunt and uncle didn't suffer from compassion fatigue, because to them, it was really just a business. But it was more than that to Heidi. When she reflects on that time in her life, she feels overwhelming exhaustion and frustration. So when she left Nebraska for college, the last thing she wanted to do was to work with animals ever again—even though it was her greatest joy. Looking back, she sees this was compassion fatigue. She had never been able to stop feeling for the cattle, and it had taken a steep toll.

Though the vet professionals she works with operate in a very different context than a cattle ranch, their compassion fatigue looks similar to what she experienced. One of her biggest goals with her vets is to help them avoid riding the highs and lows too hard. You can't let the highs—of, say, the successful births of a bunch of puppies—be too high, or you'll come crashing down when one of the litter dies. Absolutely you should feel the joy, and feel the despair, she says, but try to keep the swings from going so far in either direction. Talking to a team of colleagues is one of the best ways to help you moderate those swings, as you're able to normalize the highs and lows, to see that everyone has them, and to see that you are part of a team so the wins and losses are collective. And you need to take time away.

Sometimes people work for ages at calibrating their emotions around animal-welfare work, but the compassion fatigue doesn't get any better. Again, it's not going to go away completely, but it needs to be manageable. I know this happened to people on my team at the shelter, and I know it happens to people I go out on the streets with. It sometimes happens that the person recognizes they can't work in the industry. It's just too painful for them. And that's fine, too. Everyone needs to know their limits and use their time, talents, and compassion in a sustainable way. It's a message I repeat to myself all the time.

* * *

I've figured out my own way to calibrate. It's taken me years, but I know when I'm burning out and need to pull back. I'll leave Skid Row and go to my fancy gym on the water to work out, and I don't feel guilty about it at all. This respite allows me to get back out there the next day, and the day after that. Exercise has always been a release for me, and I know it's one of the best tools to combat depression. I'm lucky, too, because my dad passed his athleticism on to me.

Exercise isn't a cure-all but it helps me reset. I also know when I've pulled back too far and need to lean in. If I've been away from the streets too long, I get a sort of itch. Like my heart knows it needs to give more in order to feel whole.

It was hardest to find this calibration in the shelter. It was just so busy, all the time, that caring for myself and being strategic about my longevity in the job took discipline. I'd take off for walks sometimes, but more often, I had another way to recharge.

My staff didn't know this, but when I was feeling particularly tired or low, I'd go back to where the dog kennel runs were and crawl into one to play with a dog for a while. I'd pick a kennel without a lot of foot traffic so people wouldn't see me. Then after about ten minutes, I'd get up, brush off, and go back into the main clinic without anyone knowing where I'd been or why. It seems silly that I was so secretive about it. Partly, I think I wanted to always seem like the put-together general to Paisley's sergeant. If they saw me playing with a pup like I was a seven-year-old, I worried it would compromise my authority. But mainly, I think I just wanted to keep things simple, to have a private interaction with a dog that was separate from my role as doctor.

The kennels were ten feet tall, so there was a good amount of room to play. I'd crouch and let the dog bounce around me and lick my bald head. I'd play tug-of-war, toss a ball, or tussle around with them for a while. Sure, it was good for the dog. But it was also good for me. I had my own therapy dogs at my disposal, anytime I needed one.

I never liked to show that I had favorites, but there was one dog I really bonded with. It was an adorable lab-pit mix, less than a year old, grayish, with white boots on its feet. When I got in the kennel with him, he'd start doing the helicopter thing dogs do, circling me and sticking his butt in the air in the universal language of "let's play!" He had so much energy and was eager to please me so that I'd stay and play with him some more. I kept going back to his kennel, day after day.

This dog reached his two-week shelter limit and was automatically placed on the euthanasia list. But I knew this was an adoptable dog—he just needed more time. So I took him off—something I always had the authority to do but needed to be restrained about. Another week passed and he showed up on the euthanasia list again. And again, I took him off. Right at the end of that next week, right when he was going to come on the list again, he got adopted by a wonderful family.

The next week, when I needed a break, I slipped away from my desk and into the kennel of another dog. And on and on it went.

These moments in the kennels were my time to just be a pet lover, to simply be around a cool, loving dog for a little bit, to toss a ball around or play to release some steam. In these moments, I was like a kid again. And then I could leave and go back to the work at hand.

Chapter 7

WHEN IT ALL
COMES TOGETHER

One of my vet school professors told us, "One day you're going to have this amazing moment where it will feel like God has whispered in your ear. You'll be out and working, and you still won't feel like you know what you're doing, but then there will be a moment when it all comes together. When everything you learn just fits into place, and you realize you know what you're doing."

I had that moment when I was about ten months into my first job at a clinic in San Diego. It was a random day, a random case, and suddenly the lightbulb went on, and I realized, *I get it*. It all came together. And ironically, this is also around the time it all fell apart.

That first job paid me $48,000 a year, and I thought I had it made. I'd studied and worked minimum-wage jobs for most of my life, starting with flipping burgers at McDonald's for $3.15 an hour. (I'm still a grill wizard because of that experience, and it was my pizza delivery job that paid for Baron.) So $48,000 seemed like a huge amount of money. I had pinched pennies for years, and finally, for the first time, I didn't have to. I bought my dream car, a brand-new Mustang Cobra that I drove right off the showroom floor. It was exhilarating to point and say, "I want that one," and then to drive off the lot with it.

I started dating a woman, Trinity, around this time. I first noticed her when I was at a bar with my friend Teresa watching *Sunday Night Football*. Teresa tilted her head at the young couple seated next to us. "Look," Teresa nodded. "I think they're on a first date."

I glanced over and laughed. "Yeah, so awkward. She's kind of cute, though."

"Ohhhh," said Teresa. "Okay then, if the guy gets up and goes to the bathroom, I'm going to go tell her you think she's hot."

"You will not," I warned. "They're on a date!"

When later the guy got up and left the table for a minute, Teresa gestured the woman over. I squeezed Teresa's leg in warning, but she always talked a bigger game than she walked, so I wasn't too worried.

"Hey," Teresa said when she came over. "You guys on a first date?"

"Uh, yeah."

"So, how's it going?"

"Okay, I guess. He's pretty nice."

"Nice," Teresa said. She grinned mischievously. "Well, have fun."

The woman and I smiled at each other, and that was that. Until a few weeks later, when I was with a group at a booth at Denny's at 2 a.m. (a theme in my life, I guess), and I spotted her walking outside with her own clique. She saw me through the window and knocked. "Don't I know you?" she mouthed.

I went outside to talk to her. She had just moved to San Diego, too, from a small agricultural town called Modesto in the Central Valley. She worked as a waitress in a Mexican restaurant but spent most of her time exploring her new home. I knew immediately that I wanted to explore it with her. We exchanged numbers, and that was that. Trinity and I spent most of the next six months together, and then she moved in.

I was in love, I was driving a brand-new car through a city I'd always wanted to live in, and I was working in my dream job.

I thought I had it all, that life was great and always would be.

But I also had nearly $200,000 in student debt. At first, I was conscientious about it, paying my loan down by $600 a month, every month. But soon I found that my salary didn't stretch very far, between the car and the cost of living in San Diego, and the other expenses of a grown-up life that didn't include a half dozen roommates sharing utility payments. I'd been fiscally responsible to the extreme throughout my school years, I'd climbed a damn mountain, and I was sick of it. I wanted to coast for a while.

I decided to put my loans in forbearance—a grace period where I wouldn't have to make payments. And like magic, I had more money to burn each month. I was free, like I was one of my mom's horses, running full speed in the meadows. I felt I'd earned it, and loved stretching my legs without worrying about money for the first time in my life.

Of course, nothing is free, and forbearance comes with a cost— 7.2 percent interest, to be exact. When my "grace period" was up, my monthly payments were higher than ever and my options were fewer. Now I didn't have nearly $200,000 in student debt, I had *more than* $200,000 in debt. My lifestyle had grown more expensive during my time running in the meadows, and I'd maxed out some credit cards, then gotten some new ones. The more I borrowed, the more behind I became. I'd gone from having no means and living on ramen, to living beyond the modest means I had. I felt the weight of the debt I'd accumulated every day.

My solution was to work extra hours to try to pay my debts down. My boss was more than happy for me to sign up for the clinic's emergency shift, and I did so at every opportunity. But the problem was, I was still a relatively new vet. Everything it took a more seasoned veterinarian thirty minutes to do took me an hour. I was careful to the extreme, still terrified of screwing up, so I checked and rechecked and rechecked everything I did. I'd get to the clinic at 7:30 in the morning, start seeing cases at 8:00, and stay until 6:30 or 7:00. Then at 10 p.m., or 2:00 a.m., or 4:00 a.m., an emergency call would come in, and I'd be on the case again. I would go down to the clinic, bleary-eyed, and wear the hats of receptionist, billing department, vet tech, and emergency vet all at once. I'd be trying to place a catheter myself—never an easy task—and willing my hands not to shake. What if I made a mistake that led to an animal's suffering, or even its death? What if I did something that caused me to lose my license? How would I pay back my debt then? How would I explain to my family, friends, my classmates, that I was no longer qualified to treat animals?

I started to spin out, unable to sleep even when I had a night off, and was constantly on edge. Then I noticed I had some muscle fasciculations, or little tremors in my muscles. It started out in my feet, then I felt it in my hands and forearms. I tried not to think about it—I was too busy. But then I attended a continuing education night where the organizers quizzed us young vets on neurological diseases. "You might not see this one very often," the instructor said, "but it's often characterized by muscle fasciculations, and leads to paralysis. Does anyone know what it is?" My buddy Mike, by now a young doctor, happened to be attending with me, and while none of the vets in attendance had the answer, he did. "Yes," he offered. "It's ALS."

ALS. Amyotrophic lateral sclerosis. Lou Gehrig's disease. I knew enough about it to be terrified of it, and the second the session ended, I looked it up. Those who have ALS lose muscle control, little by little, until they can't speak, eat, or even breathe. And the symptoms begin just like mine, with muscle tremors. I thought, with dawning horror, *There's a good chance I have this.*

I made an appointment with a neurologist the next day, who was very dismissive of my concerns. I wasn't satisfied, so went to a second expert, one of the best in the nation. He was thorough to the extreme in his testing. He sat me down after a big work-up and said, "I don't know that you don't have it." To my ears, he was saying "You have it."

"Here's the thing about the disease," he said. "It progresses gradually. We need time—maybe three to six months—to see if it's getting worse. Time will tell me a lot. So I need you to come back in about three months and I'm going to run these tests again. If it shows growing muscle weakness, that's what we call pathognomonic, that's a smoking gun for a diagnosis. If nothing shows up in three months, I'll ask you to come back in three more months, just to make sure."

I couldn't even think about the three months. All I could think was that I might have three to five years to live.

"Kwane, you need to look at this differently," Trinity said. "He didn't say you have it—he's just being extra cautious. You just need to get out of your head about this. You need to keep going to the gym, you need to keep living your life so that the three months fly by."

It was good advice, but my mental health fell off a cliff within a week. I'd finally been so happy—in love with a woman, in love with work, in love with my idyllic beach lifestyle—and now it was all going to be taken from me. I would lose all of my dignity and die a slow and painful death under a mountain of debt. It's one thing, I felt, if you're running through a process to diagnose a disease that can be treated. But there's no real treatment for ALS—all you can do is slow its effects.

I didn't have enough discipline to push down my negative thoughts, and they haunted me every waking minute. Worse, I hated myself for not being able to control my mind. I wanted to be the guy Trinity had suggested I be, someone who saw the doctor, was told to come back in three months, and said, "Okay, sure. Going fishing now, see you in a few." But that wasn't me. I couldn't do it. I had trouble working—I lost focus with my patients and misdiagnosed easy things. My boss asked if I was okay, pointed out that I had a blank stare all the time. I was going to lose my job over this. Then what would happen to my debt? And did it even matter if I was going to die anyway?

That's how I found myself on Mission Beach one afternoon, sitting against a cement wall, pills in my pocket and eyes on the surf that could take me away from all of it. I thought of my first week in vet school, when we'd learned about that senior who took his own life right before entering the job of his dreams. I thought, too, of the Blues Men. Of my tight group of high school friends, three had taken their own lives: Craig, twin brother to Chris; Scott, the redhead who was shark bait until our group swept in and the safety of numbers shielded him; and Rab, whose intelligence far exceeded that of anyone else in the group. That made three out of seven. Even then, that statistic shook me. What was it about Albuquerque? Or was it something about being a young man that just sucked so desperately that death seemed preferable? I'd mourned each of my friends, but hadn't connected their loss to my own suffering. Now I started to.

Two choices, Kwane, I thought. *Hospital or waves.* That day, I chose the hospital.

I stayed for a few days and found the doctors helpful. They taught me how to retrain some of my most destructive thoughts. They explained positive and negative feedback loops, and how to break my negative loops by talking back to some of my greatest fears. They gave me medication, they gave me some skills and some hope, and then they released me.

A few weeks later, Trinity was at her waitressing job and I was home by myself watching *Sunday Night Football*. I'd had a couple of beers, and as I watched the game, my mind started to do its thing, imagining all that could go wrong and then building on all that certainly *would* go wrong. I took a Xanax, like the hospital staff had told me to do. But I should have known better than to take one when I'd been drinking.

I called Trinity at work and said, simply, "I don't want to be here anymore."

"Stay right there, Kwane," she said. "You're okay, you're fine. I'm leaving work right now and coming home."

By the time she got home, I was crying uncontrollably. "I don't want to do this anymore, I can't handle these thoughts anymore. These thoughts are going to kill me."

I tried to leave the house, but Trinity wouldn't let me—and called 911 instead. Two police officers—a man and a woman—got there in minutes.

"On a scale of one to ten," one of the officers said once I'd shown them to the living room, "ten being suicidal, and one not at all, where are you on that scale?"

"Probably a five or a six," I answered.

The guy cop looked at his partner, then said, "Sir, we're going to have to bring you in."

"Bring me in where?" I asked, starting to panic. Did he mean jail? Or the hospital again? I didn't want to go to either.

"We're going to take you in and get you some help." The way he said it, it was clear he wasn't giving me a choice in the matter.

"No way in hell," I said. As he approached me, I put a wristlock on him and pushed him away. The female cop came in my direction, clearly thinking they'd have to double-team to subdue me, so I gave her a stiff arm on the chest. I was completely out of my mind. The male officer got his bearings and maced me. I couldn't see anything, I was swinging and panicking and I could feel him grabbing my arms. I threw him down, body-slamming him, and when the female officer grabbed my shoulder, I shook her off. It got nasty, with Trinity yelling and crying in the background, but the officer team finally pinned me down on the ground, cuffed me, and got me into the back of the police car. I was lying on my back, but at six-three, my head was against one window and my legs up on the other.

The police left me there while they went back into the apartment to talk to Trinity. I took the opportunity to smash out the glass in the window with my feet, and started inching myself out of the car. The male officer came running and pushed me back in. "We have to go *now!*" he shouted to his partner, and the next thing I knew I was in a hospital bed and given an injection.

I think I blacked out for a bit, but then I felt calmer. A therapist came to talk to me. My ankles and wrists were strapped down. The therapist, in a nice, gentle voice, said, "Let's talk about what's going on with you. How are you feeling?"

"I'm okay," I said. "I feel better." In reality, I didn't, but I knew I needed to talk her down. "But my eyes are stinging from the mace," I explained. "Can my hands be free for a minute so I can wipe them? Having them strapped down is making me more anxious."

She agreed, and unstrapped just one of my hands, which I used to wipe my eyes, then placed it calmly on my chest and closed my eyes. The second the therapist walked away, I used my free hand to start unstrapping the rest of the restraints. The male officer must have been posted right outside the curtain, because when he heard the commotion, he came right in, but he was too late—I'd pulled off all my restraints.

"Sir—" he began, and started moving toward me.

I wrapped my hand around his throat and lifted him off his feet. In seconds, I got tackled by a bunch of people—orderlies and nurses and I don't know who else. Then someone injected me with something really strong, and I woke up the next morning.

I was horrified when all that I'd done the previous night came back to me. I thought of all I'd put everyone through—Trinity, of course, but especially that male officer. I asked the nurse on duty if he was okay.

"Yeah," he said. "I talked to him after everything calmed down. He felt really bad for you. He's not going to press charges." That's when it hit me that I had assaulted a police officer. "He could tell you were hurting," the nurse continued, "and he doesn't want to add to your problems." Tears filled my eyes—of relief, of shame, and mostly of gratitude. I've never looked at police officers the same way since he granted me that kindness.

My mom flew in from New Mexico as I remained involuntarily admitted. I stayed for five days and spent most of my time looking out this tiny window in a cinder-block building. It might not have been jail, but it felt like it. I got thirty minutes a day to spend in a common area, where I watched an older guy talking to himself and air boxing, and an older woman talking to a rock like it was a baby. It hit me just how essential it was for me to get my shit together. Forget my aspirational vision of the guy who gets scary medical news and shrugs and goes fishing. That wasn't going to be me. But I needed to *not* be the guy talking to himself and air boxing all day. I complied with everything the doctors told me to do. I took all the meds and attended all the sessions they recommended with psychologists and psychiatrists.

A few weeks later, it was time for my three-month check-in with the neurologist. Trinity went with me, and I think she must have talked to the doctor about what I'd been through since I'd last seen him, because he was very gentle and encouraging. My muscle function hadn't decreased, he explained, and more than likely I had always had some muscle tremors but hadn't noticed them. The next three months until my next meeting with him *did* pass quickly, and in the end, I was cleared of ALS risk.

While my breakdown happened some twenty years ago, some things never left me from that awful time. The compassion shown to me by that police officer remains paramount. But so does a visceral sense of how close I came to the edge—or rather, how close I came to not clawing my way back. I made a few bad financial decisions when I didn't know better, and it kicked off a negative spiral. I worked many more hours than I should have, sacrificing sacred and necessary sleep, which made the anxiety of my job, the fear of screwing up, impossible to put in perspective. Equally out of perspective was my fear of disease and death. I made a dumb choice one night to take a Xanax when I'd had some beer, and I could have hurt someone much worse than I did, or I could have taken my life.

But the greatest lesson from that time underpins the very way I move throughout the world now: Sometimes the most coveted markers of a "good" life—prestigious school, good job, new car, beach town, girlfriend—don't mean much at all. Sometimes they actually bind you. I'll never forget that recognition I had on the beach about how pointless my climb had been. And I'll never forget how, when you are hurting and just want free of it all, you can go into the waves, as I considered doing—or you can decide to live life on your own terms, society be damned.

* * *

My phone buzzed one afternoon, and I was surprised to see the number. Why was Daren calling me? I'd just seen him. Daren typically camped on a patch of grass near Universal Studios with his cat, Buddha the Wanderer. Buddha was healthy, his fleas were well handled, and I'd answered all of Daren's questions when I'd stopped in to do an exam just days ago.

The strain in Daren's voice said it all. "Dr. K, can you come quick? A car just hit Buddha! He's been hit," he repeated. "He's hurt real bad, I think."

"I'll be right there," I said. "Just don't move." As I sat through LA's miserable traffic, I worried. While I would wake up plenty of nights worried about homeless people I'd met, Daren had never been one of them. Unlike others who were desperate to get off the streets, Daren enjoyed his lifestyle and was happy-go-lucky about seemingly everything. But this cat was decidedly not just a pet to him. From what I could tell, Daren was friendly with everyone but didn't have close and consistent friends. Buddha was Daren's family. Buddha was Daren's *home*.

As I sat bumper to bumper, nervous about what I might find when I arrived, my mind wandered to the moment we met.

Daren's the kind of guy you notice right away. He's tall and thin, and has an easygoing smile, surrounded by thick blondish stubble. His skin is damaged from spending all of his time outside, so it's hard to pinpoint his age, but I'd put him in his early thirties. He could often be seen skateboarding around Venice Beach, with a pack piled high on his back, and several duffel bags slung across his body. It's an impressive balance feat, to be honest—like if the Tower of Pisa were on roller skates. But what really makes Daren hard to miss is the cat perched atop his shoulders as he rides.

Buddha is a long-haired calico cat with sharp green eyes. They met when Daren heard meowing in a dumpster one day and stopped to investigate. He was just a kitten then, and while we don't know Buddha's origin story, I'd worked at a shelter long enough to know what it likely was.

When the days get longer, felines start breeding. It's an instinctual evolutionary thing. When I'd worked at the shelter, from March to June, multiple cardboard boxes of kitten litters were dropped on our doorstep daily. Many sickly starving strays from cat colonies, which desperately needed to be nursed six or seven times a day. I just didn't have the manpower to bottle-feed them all that frequently. On some spring days I would have to euthanize up to forty or fifty kittens. The ones who didn't come into the shelter ended up hungry, and if they survived long enough, they made their way to dumpsters and alleys searching for scraps. That's where Buddha and Daren found each other.

Daren had been on the road awhile already when he met Buddha. He was unapologetic about his lifestyle, calling himself a nomad, but I knew there was more to the story. He was originally from Arkansas, and though we didn't talk about it much, I gathered something went very wrong in his home state. All he said was that he left it after he had a falling-out with family members and lost his construction job. A life on the road, he decided, fit him just fine.

He felt more comfortable out in the elements than anywhere else, which I learned after I offered to let him stay at my apartment once when I was going to be away. I showed him around and told him to make himself comfortable, to do his laundry, take a shower, get some good sleep. He looked like a kid dressed up for church but who'd much rather be climbing trees. Later, I got a call from the building security guard. "There's a guy wandering around the grounds," he said. "He's just kind of . . . meandering. Says he's a guest of yours?" I assured him he was. Daren just couldn't be still. This was just Daren being Daren. He was a traveler.

Daren had seen much more of the country than I ever will. Before California, he'd been to North Carolina, Wisconsin, Illinois, Missouri, Texas, Wyoming, Colorado, New Mexico, Oregon, and Washington—just to name a few. Unlike many of the other people I met, he was not looking for transitional housing. I often wondered how he got by, and got an inkling when, after one meeting, I asked if I could come check up on Buddha in a couple of days.

"Yeah, yeah," he said. "I'm taking off for a bit, but I'll be back. I've got to go to Vegas."

"Yeah? Why's that?"

"Oh," he said with nonchalance, "someone gave me this ticket for forty-five dollars and I just have to redeem it at the Rio. So me and Buddha are going to make our way out to Vegas to get it."

"Isn't that a bit of a hassle?" I asked him, almost laughing. "I mean, aren't you going to spend the forty-five dollars just to get to Vegas, only to have to come right back?"

"Nah, man, it's good," he said. He would travel the nearly three hundred miles through a combination of skateboarding, hitchhiking, and taking the bus. But it was no big deal. He reassured me it made good sense, and that it wasn't a hassle, but a fun trip where he'd get to meet some new people, skateboard in some cool places, and show Buddha some different sites.

That pretty much summed up Daren. Not much was a big deal to him, and he didn't want any pity. He loved being able to switch locales at a moment's notice, and there was no such thing as an ordeal—it was all about the experience. He and Buddha slept in a tent that wouldn't close ever since the zipper broke, but he shrugged it off, explaining he used paper clips when it got windy. It was all part of life on the open road. The only thing that was hard for him about his nomadic existence, he said, was that it could be lonely. That's why he had Buddha. "All I need is a companion," he said.

Such is the traveler's story. "It is some years," wrote John Steinbeck in his memoir about driving solo around the United States, *Travels with Charley*, "since I have been alone, nameless, friendless, without any of the safety one gets from family, friends, and accomplices. . . . It's just a very lonely, helpless feeling at first—a kind of desolate feeling. For this reason I took one companion on my journey—an old French gentleman poodle known as Charley." Steinbeck knew, as Daren did, that he needed a witness to his adventures. He needed continuity alongside constant motion. Who better to serve that role than an animal?

Dogs have served the Charley role for centuries, of course, but Daren didn't have a dog. He had a Buddha. As much as I loved Sushi, and as big of a cat person as I am, even I can see that they do not always make the most loyal companions. "Cats," one of my vet school professors had seared into students' brains, "are not small dogs."

Medically, that's obviously true (they have a remarkably different physiology and as a result have different diseases and treatment). And just as obvious behaviorally: they want to take life on their time. The more we try to make them conform to what we want, the more their ears slouch down as they offer a death stare. No one can say *What do you think you're doing?* with a mere look quite like a pissed-off cat. This doesn't mean they're not incredibly intelligent or just as trainable as dogs. They're not far descended from the big cats you see in circus acts and that I saw trained for movies.

But cats are not going to give you something for nothing, and they're not unique in that. Dogs, in fact, are the only domesticated animal who will respond to affection as a training reward. Cats would like their treat, please and thank you and goodbye, and it had better be more than a scratch under the chin.

Daren and Buddha broke the mold on the human-cat bond. First of all, the skateboarding. Dogs might love to ride in moving vehicles and feel the wind on their face, but cats? Usually they loathe it. They're famous for hating cars. They like to be perched high, but rolling fast, without control, down a street? No way. And yet that's exactly what Daren trained Buddha to do. Teaching Buddha to skateboard was, like everything, no big deal. "I taught him to ride on my shoulders when he was just a kitten," he shrugged. "I took him to a Walmart parking lot and skated around it constantly. It took a few days but he got used to it. Now it's his safe spot."

Typically, cats like to be with their owners, but they also love to be out on their own, stalking prey like their forebears. But Buddha was with Daren constantly. "He's my baby," Daren said. "He's the best thing I've ever had. He gives me pancakes on my chest. He cuddles with me, he sleeps with me at night." Daren would read in his tent for hours, with Buddha curled into his side, head perched just above Daren's armpit.

They made quite the impression—the happy-go-lucky skateboarding nomad and the cat who was content to go along for the ride.

* * *

When I got to Daren, he was beside himself. He was holding Buddha, but couldn't bring himself to look at him. I'd seen this reaction from owners before, and suspected he was afraid to inspect him, or to see the signs of his suffering. I took Buddha right away and tried to get Daren moving, but it was like Daren had been stunned. "We've got to go, man, pack up," I said. He looked at me blankly. "C'mon, man, let's get moving. We need to get Buddha to the hospital." Daren moved like he was walking underwater, and kept telling Buddha, "I'm so sorry, baby."

I was worried about Buddha's breathing. I suspected a couple of his ribs were broken, and he was likely in shock, but I didn't know how bad it was, nor would I until we got an X-ray. I wrapped him up in blankets and we left for Beverly Oaks Animal Hospital, where I'd call for help from Dr. Leach and Dr. Pedraza once again.

We stabilized Buddha and did an X-ray, which made it very clear the internal damage to this poor cat was extensive. If he lived through the night, he would need surgery to repair his diaphragm, which had been ruptured, causing his intestines to move up into his chest. One of his back legs was also broken, and he'd need metal pins placed inside it so he'd have use of it again. Buddha might make it through, but there were a lot of "ifs." It was going to be a long night.

Daren waited on the sidewalk outside the clinic, alternately pacing and weeping, as we examined Buddha. He put his hands over his mouth as I explained how touch-and-go the next twenty-four hours would be, and he moaned, though he tried to stifle it. He blamed himself for Buddha getting hit, even though there was nothing he could have done to prevent it.

He wanted to say good night to Buddha, who was heavily sedated. He wiped his eyes as we opened the cage where Buddha was resting, a tube in his mouth to help him breathe. Daren came undone. "I'm so sorry, baby." Daren cried and stroked Buddha's nose. "I love you."

After Daren left, Dr. Pedraza and I had much more to talk about. If Buddha were to survive the night and be eligible for surgery, it would not be cheap. When pets get hurt, owners are shocked about the expense. Just coming in the door and having vet staff start the stabilization process for an injured animal can rise to $2,000–$3,000. It's not something the average working person can afford, let alone a homeless person. Then, in Buddha's case, there was the cost of anesthesia, surgery, a titanium plate for his leg, and the twelve days or so of hospitalization he would require. In fact, market rate for Buddha's treatment would exceed $10,000. It wasn't a matter of the value of my time, which I was happy to volunteer. But I'm not an animal surgeon—Buddha required specialized, highly skilled care. For comparison on the human side, the same treatment would be $200,000–$250,000 before insurance. Thanks to the generosity of Dr. Pedraza and Dr. Leach, we were able to get costs down, but there were still costs. Daren's clear distress convinced us we had to make this surgery happen, and we all—from Dr. Pedraza to the vet tech—pitched in money and time.

When people hear this story, they often give me the side-eye. They're well-meaning, practical, bighearted people, and they explain they are also really confused. Usually the conversation goes something like this: "We have so many problems in the world, Kwane. *Daren* has so many problems. That kind of money could pay for a year's worth of housing. It could pay to buy food for hungry pets, not to mention hungry people. How can you justify this?"

I'm the last person to be divorced from hard, practical realities. You can't turn away from problems of scale when you're responsible for as many as four hundred animals a day, as I was at the Stanislaus County shelter. I had so often wished there was an algorithm, or a hard-line rule to tell me when an animal had to be put down and that my judgment was inconsequential. But that wasn't how it worked at all. I had to weigh risks and benefits constantly, and I had exclusive power to take an animal off the euthanasia list. I sometimes did, to spare myself and the staff the heartbreak. But then I'd come in to work the next morning to find animal control had brought in a stray puppy, and because of the choice I'd made to save another animal, we had no room for him. The fact that I had so much discretion was the worst part of my job. My philosophy changed over time, though. I realized that it kept me going to have a case every week or two that reminded me I had the power to save a life that wasn't meant to be saved. If my power was the worst part of my job, I needed to make it the best part of my job, too.

Truth be told, most owners who bring a cat in in the condition

Buddha was in wouldn't be willing—or able—to pay for his surgery, and he'd be euthanized. So, in dollars and cents, no, saving Buddha wasn't the most efficient thing to do. But I do know that saving Buddha recognized the humanity in me. And raising the money to save Buddha made me, Dr. Leach, and Dr. Pedraza recommit to being healers, first and foremost.

It also recognized the humanity in Daren. By valuing his animal that was so precious to him, we were telling him we valued him.

* * *

Luckily, Buddha survived the night. I didn't have much of a role in the surgery when it happened the next morning. Dr. Pedraza was the best animal surgeon in Los Angeles, and the best role I could serve was as a comfort to Daren, who was a mess during the days of Buddha's recovery. He wanted to sleep outside the vet hospital, but wouldn't come inside to see Buddha. He'd been too overcome by seeing Buddha so compromised that first night. Some days he said, "Okay, I want to come in and see him," only to decide he just couldn't do it.

After twelve days, though, Buddha was ready to go. It's pretty remarkable when you think about it—a surgery so invasive and serious, and it took less than two weeks for this cat to get back to normal. In the animal world, cats are known for having superpowers, like they're carrying around some amazing healing serum. In vet school we had a saying: "To get a cat's broken leg *not* to heal, you have to hide it from them." Seriously. I've seen the most crazy dislocated fractures in cats, where the owner didn't do any work to help it heal.

It might not have healed *correctly*, but it healed. That just doesn't happen with people or dogs.

When Daren came inside the clinic for the first time since before the surgery, he was still fearful. He put his hands back over his mouth as we walked to Buddha's crate. But Buddha was not only a traveling, skateboarding cat, he was a credit to his species' healing capabilities. He was back to normal and quick to purr and jump back on Daren's shoulders. Daren smiled for the first time in two weeks. He left the clinic that day with a tag for Buddha, announcing him as "Buddha the Wanderer."

Their story doesn't end with "So Daren found a great job, an apartment, and a girlfriend who had her own cat, so now Buddha is also a proud father of a litter of kittens." This isn't a Disney movie, and that ending would probably sound horrific to Daren anyway. The last I heard from him, Daren and Buddha were in the Bay Area. Daren still checks in with me periodically. His number will pop up on my phone and he'll jump into "Dr. K, Buddha's been itching," or "Dr. K, Buddha's got this stuff on his ear," as if not a day has passed, and as if he's a regular client. Which, in the end, I guess he is.

* * *

Kate lived with her midsized mutt, Poppa, on the streets in downtown San Diego. It was clear from just a moment talking to Kate, who held court in her tent, that she had some significant physical difficulties. She might have been in her fifties or sixties, though it was hard to tell. Her tear ducts were clogged up, which made her eyes look irritated, and her speech was quiet and hard to follow. But she had a lot to say.

She'd grown up in Massachusetts, and though she didn't get into the specifics of her life, she explained that she'd survived things most people wouldn't, including a serious lung disease. She lived for a time out in the woods, where she helped take care of a neighbor's bull mastiff. She'd always gravitated to dogs, she said, and to kids, because "they're genuine and they don't pull any punches." The more we talked, the clearer it became that Kate was a bit of an institution on the block. Several people stopped by during our visit to give me the side-eye and say, "Aunty, all okay here?"

She told them yes each time, then explained to me that the respect she got was due to her longevity. She'd lived on the block for nineteen years—some of it in a nearby apartment, but most of it on the streets. She'd walked those same streets for nights on end when she suffered from insomnia. "A lot of people out here call me Aunty or Momma," she said. "I find that the younger generation, they ask me questions about how to handle different things. I tell them that you don't always have to fight fire with fire. Sometimes you can use a squirt bottle."

"How do you get by?" I asked, surprised that she could keep the lifestyle going for so long. I'd met people who had lived on the streets for a few years, but nineteen? That was a new record.

"By hustling." She shrugged.

"But how do you hustle?"

"I don't know! I just hustle!" It was clear that conversation thread was done.

Poppa, she explained, claimed Kate as an owner and not the other way around. Poppa had been with an owner who abused him, and somehow Kate's brother got wind of what was going on and asked if he could give the dog to Kate. "He listened immediately to the commands I gave him," Kate said of their first meeting. And then, that was that. Poppa was Kate's dog. "He's the part of me that nobody sees. He displays all my opposites. I'm not a people person but he loves attention." Kate and Poppa were rarely apart after that, except for a few days when Kate's son passed away. "He wouldn't eat anything when I was gone. I came back and got him and he ate right away."

Kate and Poppa sometimes stayed in a hotel for a few nights, but mostly, they set up camp on the street. "This is where I want to be," Kate said. "This is a choice. It wasn't because I had to be out here, it's because I needed to be out here. I wanted to live life on my own terms and this is as close to freedom as I'll ever get. And I am living life on my own terms."

The bathroom situation, she acknowledged, was annoying, but other than that she had no complaints. "It's not hard for me. It's harder for people who see me and say, 'you have so much potential.' And I say, 'I'm glad you see that in me. But where I was, I wasn't happy.' I was always stressed out and worried what other people thought of me."

I could see Kate —and the block she lived on—the way the business owners and local residents must have. Trash was strewn everywhere, as was food residue that attracted bugs and undoubtedly rodents. It smelled—not as bad as Skid Row, but you were never far from a whiff of urine. It wasn't sanitary, and it was unquestionably ugly. It's one thing to see the homeless and feel frustrated that affordable housing and social services aren't available to them, if that's the case. But it's another thing when those services *are* available to them, but they say "no, thank you." Plenty of people will disagree with me on either side of this issue, but my feeling is that we live in a society, and a community, and we've got to honor that we can't just do whatever we want wherever we want.

At the same time, there's a strong core in me that wishes there was more room for alternative lifestyles, and that wonders where all these rules came from in the first place. When Kate talked about being removed from the trappings of a more traditional life, or when Daren talked about wanting to be free to hop a bus to Vegas at a moment's notice, part of me wanted that, too.

When I first met Daren, I'd look at him and think, *Why don't you get a car? Why don't you work?* But then I thought back to my breakdown in my twenties and wondered, *Why do I think that?* The truth was, Daren was happy. In many ways I envied him; he wasn't worried about paying his utility bill the way I was, or whether he'd made the right call about saving an animal, or whether or not he'd remembered to take out the garbage or turn off the coffeepot. He had few possessions or responsibilities. He got to live in the moment the way the rest of us have to download an app to do. All of these things were true for Kate, too. Give them a blanket, and a furry companion, and they're good.

Maybe they were the ones who had it right, and we were the ones who had it wrong.

Rob, my high school buddy and English-class defender, had gone a different route, too. He remains whip-smart, and I've still never beaten the guy in an argument. He could have done whatever he wanted with his life. His brother and sister left Albuquerque and went on to really illustrious, high-profile careers in business and law. Rob could have, too. But he loved music and hated being told what to do by anyone. So he moved to Seattle, where he could play guitar in a band. He started a pool-cleaning company (yep, in Seattle—not exactly California, where pools punctuate the majority of backyards) and he still spends his days cleaning pools. People could say "Dude, you wasted a life. You wasted a brain." But I'm not so sure. Not when I think about our group of Blues Men, and how we lost Craig, Scott, and Rab. When I think of the loss of their lives, I think of waste. When I think about how Rob's living his, I think, what's wasteful about being happy?

Because the reality is that Rob is doing great. He *is* happy. He plays his guitar, and no one tells him what to do. He's living by his own rules. Like Kate said, it's harder for other people who look and see wasted potential than it is for him to live life how he wants to. That's not waste, it's freedom.

Chapter 8

AN IMPOSSIBLE CHOICE

After everything Trinity and I had been through together, proposing to her was the easiest decision of my life. We got married, and when I'd just turned thirty, we had a baby boy. Trinity's pregnancy and labor went smoothly, and the moment the baby came out, Trinity's friend Jessica—who was on hand for support—tried to take a photo. But an entire team of people rushed into the room, including a doctor who looked like he'd just woken up, and told Jessica to move aside as they swooped the baby onto a special table.

Trinity started crying and asking what was going on. "We're just trying to clear his throat," someone said. Someone else gestured for me to stand in a corner of the room. I did exactly what they said. I was deeply worried and entered a sort of shut-down mode. I'd also been the doctor in emergency situations and knew how much concentration was required in moments like this one. The last thing you want when you're up at the plate, waiting for a fast pitch, is for someone to be blowing in your ear.

Not that I blamed Trinity for her very verbal panic. "Hold on, ma'am, please just hold on," was all the doctors said. She'd just birthed her first child and five, ten, fifteen minutes passed without her being able to hold him or know what was going on.

Then at last they handed him to her and explained there had been an issue with his airway, and that he hadn't been getting enough oxygen. They'd want him to stay in the NICU for a few days, they explained, just to make sure, but she could hold him and nurse him.

Six hours after Kamon was born, the three of us were in a normal hospital room, and the nurse came in to check on him. The nurse pulled the blanket away from where Trinity had been cradling him and looked at his tiny face, then turned to look at me. "Ohhhh," she cooed. "You look just like your daddy."

The past few hours had been so stressful I hadn't let the elation hit me. With this nurse's comment, it did. This was my Lion King moment. This was my son.

We had wanted a name that started with "K," and when I thought of Kamon, Trinity was immediately on board. The day we got to take him home, I remember approaching our front door and thinking with wonder, "There are three of us now. We're a family of three."

* * *

Barbara was the proud owner of two cockatoos, Boo Boo and Jericho. She'd had them from the time they were eggs, and when I met them they were around thirty years old. (Cockatoos live to be sixty, eighty, or even a hundred.) Barbara never married—or rather, she did briefly but had it annulled—and never had children, which, she said, would have been selfish of her. "And anyway," she explained, "my birds are my kids." In their thirty years together, the three have formed a tight family. Barbara's voice mail chirped, "You've reached the line for Barbara, Boo Boo, and Jericho."

Barbara lived in transitional housing when I met her. I immediately liked her "kids"—Boo Boo and Jericho were playful birds who loved to bop up and down, dancing and showing off for me. They say "Hello" and "Goodbye" as the basics, but also "Whatcha doing?" and "Close that damn door!" and "I love you." "People don't think birds have personalities," Barbara explained, "and they do. People don't think that they cuddle, and they do. They come right up my legs and up on my chest." Barbara was in her sixties, and was thin, with wispy gray hair beneath a knitted beanie. She wore small round glasses and had a huge laugh she let out almost like it was punctuation. She smiled all the time, made friends easily, and fit every description you can imagine of "bird lady." Minus the birds, she actually reminded me a lot of my grandma, who would wave enthusiastically in the exact same way, and laugh at almost everything I said, even when I knew it wasn't very funny—she was just delighted by everything because she was delighted by life.

Barbara grew up on Castle Air Force Base near Merced, California, and her love affair with birds began when her mother gave her a parakeet, Blue Boy, when she was five years old. While she had a dog once, a Rottweiler, mostly he just served as transportation and entertainment for her true love, cockatoos.

For years, Barbara would travel around the country with Boo Boo and Jericho, hitchhiking or taking the bus to see friends in other states, staying at inexpensive hotels along the way. "One time," she told me, "I was sitting waiting for the bus and I guess someone thought I was homeless and they called the cops. And the cops ended up giving me a ride to where I needed to go!" She laughed her big laugh. "So there's all kinds of nice little things."

That said, Barbara *has* been homeless, and it was not an experience she would ever want to repeat. She'd been living in West Covina, just outside Los Angeles, and breeding tropical birds. Life was pretty good, and Boo Boo and Jericho were beloved in the town. Locals got accustomed to seeing Barbara walking down the street, her parrots perched on her shoulder or her walker. The birds called greetings out to everyone they passed, and even became the unofficial mascots of the Covina Police Department for a time. Then, one night, Barbara and a group of friends were about to sit down for cake and ice cream, when an electrical fire broke out. Barbara got everyone out and saved Boo Boo and Jericho. But she lost seventy-five birds, and her home, in the fire.

The Salvation Army gave her a week's stay in a hotel to figure out her next steps. But with two birds, and no insurance, and the loss of the birds that had been her livelihood, she had no place to go. She stayed with different friends, but the noise and mess from the birds was always too much for them, and she had to move on. The thing about Boo Boo and Jericho is they're noisy. Cockatoos are the loudest of all parrots—they enjoy making a racket and will scream at each other or at people to communicate, and to remind you that they're there and to *please pay attention to me!* "When they want attention," Barbara said, "they yell and scream like they are now."

So, yeah. They don't make for the best roommates. Even in the late nineteenth century, they were known as a pain in the ass. The academic Katherine Grier found letters from the period from a guy named John Gould—who generally liked animals—who hatched a plot to kill his mother-in-law's parrot (named Polly, because of course). He wrote to his housekeeper about the animal's upcoming visit, "I would give $5.00 gladly [if] the D-/ beast would die or be found so by any means. A bunch of Parsley a pin in her back or a Brick or flat Iron dropped on her. If you can accomplish this I will send you the above amount only keep it to yourself . . ."[*]

So far as she knows, no one has ever plotted to kill Barbara's birds, but no one welcomed them, either. When Barbara ran out of her friends' goodwill, she and her birds moved outside. They were homeless for two and a half years. On the bright side, she would go down to Santa Monica Pier and let tourists take pictures with her and the birds, and made pretty good money that way. In just four hours on a weekend, she could make as much as $200. She loved showing off her birds to people, but hated sleeping outdoors.

"Sometimes we slept on the street," she said, "on porches, and in carports around Santa Monica. It was horrible. I didn't know where I was going to stay or what I was going to do. Thank God I'm strong and I survived it. It was so hard to be homeless with them. I had a walker and they knew to stay on the walker. But I had some times where people tried to steal my birds off me when I was sleeping."

Barbara had people who cared for her, though. A cop in the area had a cockatoo and would always come check up on them and drop off big bags of birdseed. So would a fireman who had a cockatoo.

---

[*] Katherine C. Grier, *Pets in America: A History* (Chapel Hill: Univ. of North Carolina Press, 2006), 52.

"They looked out for me," she said, and even did extra rounds to check on her. Once she was walking down the Santa Monica promenade, a famous pedestrian shopping street, and a guy tripped her. Before she could pick herself up off the ground, the man was reaching for her birds. "But there was a cop around the corner who saw what he was trying to do," Barbara told me smugly, "and arrested him."

Her birds may have made living on the streets tough, but they also made it bearable. Barbara has suffered from anxiety for much of her life, and when she feels a panic attack coming on, her birds know it almost before she does. "They just sense it. They just know. They come and play with me and my anxiety goes down. They start talking to me, saying, 'Hi, Barbara! Whatcha doing? I'm a good boy. I love you.'"

When I met Barbara, she was working on finding a permanent address for her and her birds. She needed to be out of town for a few days to look for apartments, which meant she had to board them. That was fine—she'd saved up to cover the boarding expenses. The only problem was Boo Boo and Jericho needed to be checked out by an avian veterinarian first, to make sure they didn't have any infectious diseases.

I have little experience with birds, so I couldn't be of much help. My buddy Evan Antin, however, is an exotic animal vet and offered to step in. Barbara and I took the birds to his Ventura County vet clinic, and, as I assisted him, I saw why avian vet care is so expensive. Birds are really delicate creatures, and to draw blood from one takes skill and patience. We couldn't draw blood from Boo Boo's neck vein, as we'd intended, and had to use a wing instead. You also have to be incredibly careful, because even though both parrots were really tame, if they panicked and bit me or Evan, their beaks could take off a finger.

Boo Boo and Jericho withstood the examination much better than many cockatoos would, probably because Barbara had exposed them to so many new people and situations in their lives, so nothing much threw them off. I've been on film sets before with cockatoos, and my concern is always about their stress level. For parrots and exotic birds, so many of the diseases they get are stress-related, so it's important that they stay as calm and relaxed as possible . . . for a high-maintenance animal.

Fortunately, both Boo Boo and Jericho breezed through the exam as if they had not a care in the world, and were cleared for boarding. Barbara was able to secure a permanent apartment and get back on her feet. She started to volunteer at a senior center, where she'd bring the birds and offer a presentation about their behavior and care. "Eyes just light up when people see them. And that makes me happy, that I can show off my birds to people. It makes me feel good, and it makes other people feel good." Barbara also contributes to the homeless as much as she can. She'll sometimes let them use her apartment to get cleaned up, or will buy them underwear or a pair of socks. "We've got to be easy on the homeless," she said. "They need help. Just do little things. You don't have to work at it to help the homeless. I'm on a tight budget and I still go out and give a couple of dollars here and there."

Barbara often walks to her local Dollar Tree, a trip that takes ten minutes if she doesn't have the birds, but an hour if she does. Just like when they lived in West Covina, "Everyone wants to stop and talk to me and ask me questions about my birds." Boo Boo and Jericho also have fans at the local Starbucks and a couple of nearby restaurants. "When they know I'm coming," Barbara said, "they automatically pull out the cucumbers and the grapes."

Boo Boo and Jericho have invited the curiosity and generosity of the community, but they've unquestionably made Barbara's living situation more difficult over the years. They're not easy animals—they're emotionally needy, they need a varied diet, and they want to forage for it, which often means a messy place. Their beaks can cause serious damage not just to fingers, but to doors, furniture, and door frames. The plain truth is, I can see why people might not be excited to have neighbors like Boo Boo and Jericho, and why landlords might want to avoid a tenant like Barbara. Plenty of cockatoos have been relinquished at avian rescues for this very reason.

But when I asked Barbara what she'd say to those who blame the birds for her homelessness, she said, "I'd tell them they don't know what they're talking about. I've had these birds too long. We've been through too much."

Including now, as Barbara was recently diagnosed with several different forms of cancer. "When I'm not feeling good, they come up and cuddle. They go on my chest and give me kisses while I stroke the feathers on their backs." Barbara's birds will certainly outlive her. She is thinking of leaving them to a free-flight sanctuary once she's gone, so long as they won't be separated from each other. Meanwhile, her birds are what gets her through treatments for her illness.

It's entirely possible that Barbara will lose her housing again. If she does, I have no doubt she'd go back to being homeless rather than give up her birds. And I can't say that, in her place, I'd do anything differently.

* * *

Near Venice Beach one afternoon, I met a young, fit guy named Jorge and his bull terrier, Tiny. Jorge had recently fallen on hard times and lost his housing, but he remained pretty positive. "We're having bad times now but we're going to have good times again."

I noticed right away that Tiny didn't put weight on his left front leg. Jorge said it had been messed up since he was a puppy, but that he got along well enough on three legs. Jorge pulled him around in a cart that he'd attached to his bike, and I suspected Tiny was in some pain. Jorge fell into the same camp as Walter, though, and was fearful of anything happening to Tiny in the exam room or on the operating table. He wouldn't let me take Tiny into a clinic, and his eyes reddened at the possibility. "I can't let you take my dog, man. It's deep," he said. "He's my son."

Jorge had money and could afford to live in an apartment— even in LA's competitive housing market. "No one will rent to me," he explained, "because they say, 'We need to see the dog first.'" Then, when they do, they immediately say, "Oh no, no—he's a bull terrier."

"Do they know he has just three legs?" I asked, incredulous.

Pound for pound, bull terriers have the leanest muscle of any breed, which is why they were so misused in dogfighting for so long. Target's adoption of a bull terrier mascot has unfortunately not been enough to undo the breed's reputation. But the truth about bull terriers is that they are friendly and trainable. And the fear of a bite from a dog like Tiny is completely overblown. The likelihood of being killed by a dog is roughly 1 in 18 million, and the lion's share of reported bites don't even require medical attention. In Tiny's case, he was not only docile and sweet, but again, had just *three working legs*.

Jorge was in a tough spot as he tried to navigate one bureaucratic obstacle after another while trying to work, take care of Tiny, and survive on the streets. I encouraged Jorge to go to an agency like Turning Point to help him get back on his feet. But it was a non-starter. He wouldn't get help. "I speak three languages. I have military training." His eyes teared up again. "I want to do it myself."

It's hard to get a firm figure on the number of homeless people who have animals, but estimates suggest it's around 10 percent. One thing I do know is that if we ever want to have a hope of ending—or substantially reducing—homelessness, shelters and housing options need to grasp how significant these relationships are, and that for an individual like Jorge to live within four walls, his animal has to be welcome too. Some are, and organizations like My Dog Is My Home are doing great advocacy in this area.

And still there is more work to be done. Just recently we've seen, with the war in Ukraine, the greatest refugee crisis since World War II. *The New York Times* highlighted the travails of one refugee who fled from Kyiv with her sister and her Maltese puppy. She hoped to get to friends in Virginia, a journey that took her first to Poland, then Germany, then Portugal, and then Tijuana at the Mexican border with California. Because of health regulations, she wasn't permitted to bring her dog across the border to the United States. "After their trip of more than 6,000 miles," the *Times* reported, "across four international borders, this barrier seemed the most formidable. They considered reversing their steps."[*] Luckily, a workaround presented itself. Americans *could* bring animals across the border from Mexico, and so a volunteer army popped up and crossed the border to bring the animals over.

What Barbara communicated so clearly, and what Jorge expressed, too, was that especially for people who have had their share of hardship in life, animals are not just interchangeable furry companions, they're family. I still constantly think about how Jorge put it: *It's deep. He's my son.* If I had to choose between housing and my boy? Well, what a dumb question.

---

[*] "Ukrainians Face New Hurdle at U.S. Border: No Dogs," *New York Times* (nytimes .com), April 14, 2022.

Chapter 9

BETTER MEN

I t seems to be my lot in life to have great relationships with animals, and not-as-great relationships with people. Animals come easily to me, but I'm always stepping in it when it comes to humans.

Kamon was still an infant when I fooled around with a technician at work. It was a drunken, stupid mistake, and the only consolation I have was that at least we didn't have sex. Still, I was guilt-ridden. Not only was the technician engaged, but I had a wife and baby boy at home. Trinity had been with me through my darkest hours, she'd put her body through the ringer to carry and birth our child, and she had been home taking care of him when I strayed. I hated myself, and what I'd done.

"Let it go," said the tech. "It won't happen again, and Trinity wouldn't *want* to know."

Three weeks after it happened, the guilt hadn't subsided. I kept thinking of our vows, of the ways I'd promised to be true to her. I didn't want to hurt her, but I didn't want to keep a secret like this from her, either. So I sat Trinity down one evening and said, "There's something I need to tell you."

A three-hour marathon of screaming and crying followed. "The reason I told you," I said, again, sometime in the third hour, "is that when I took our vows I meant them. I had every intention of upholding them and I think we should address what happened—I think we're strong enough to get through it. I don't want this to break us. I'll go to therapy if you want, I'll do whatever you want me to."

Trinity had calmed down by this point. "At least you didn't conceal it," she conceded, "or move on as if it was nothing."

It was 1 a.m., and we seemed to be cried out. The emotion had come down several levels and we were talking, not shouting or crying.

"I'm starving," Trinity said. "I'm going to go to Jack in the Box."

"Okay," I said, thinking we'd go to sleep once she got home.

"Do you want anything?" she asked as she walked out the door.

"Uh, sure," I said, though it felt a bit surreal. "Um, a cheeseburger and a milkshake."

She left for the restaurant that was just a few blocks away, and fifteen minutes passed. Then thirty. *That's weird*, I thought, and was just about to call her—cell phones had *just* become a thing—when she called me. She was frantic.

"Which house do they live in, Kwane? Which house is it? I know it's this cul de sac, but I don't remember which house."

Oh shit. We'd been over to the tech's house once—I couldn't believe Trinity had found her way there. *What was she doing?*

"Trinity, get in the car," I said. "Come home. Please, it's two a.m. We'll talk about it, just come home."

"If you don't tell me, Kwane, I'm going to go to every house. I'm going to confront her if it's the last thing I do."

I kept trying to talk her down, like it was a hostage situation, but soon I heard her going door to door, knocking maniacally until someone answered, then when it wasn't the right house, moving to the next one and knocking again.

Finally, I heard a female voice say, "Trinity? What are you doing here?"

Trinity let loose with a string of expletives, and all I could think was *oh shit oh shit oh shit*. Kamon was asleep—there was nothing I could do and my going over there would only make it worse. Finally I heard a door slam, and Trinity hung up.

Twenty minutes later, she came home.

"Jesus, Trinity!" I said. "What were you thinking?"

"What was *I* thinking?" she said. "What were *you* thinking, Kwane?"

We talked and cried for another hour, then finally went to sleep. In the morning, Trinity was better, and we agreed to see a marriage counselor. I reiterated again and again—with the counselor, with Trinity alone—that I was committed to making our marriage work. But from that moment on, we were irreparably broken. Weeks and months after my confession, Trinity didn't trust me to go to the gym, or go anywhere I might "find some girl."

After months of this, our marriage was over. Clearly we were not strong enough to get past it. Trinity moved back to Modesto with Kamon, so she could be close to her family.

It had all gotten so messy, and though Trinity played a part, I mostly blamed myself. I did a horrible thing to a woman who had saved my life.

My past—from my romantic life to my penchant for fighting—is clearly riddled with imperfections. And again, my overall track record with humans isn't great. I've come to realize there's an exception, though, when it comes to the people I meet in my street work. Not only do we have a deep love of animals in common, but they've been through their own versions of hell, and have made a lot of their own mistakes. I could tell them every bad thing I'd ever done, and they wouldn't judge me. They'd probably shrug and say, "It's okay. You're all right." I wouldn't get the same from some of my friends. There's an acceptance when I'm around the homeless—I accept them, and they accept me, and there's an animal between us who doesn't even understand the concept of judgment at all.

* * *

I met Don one day at Ocean Beach, in California, when I was filming some of my pet encounters for a show. I guessed Don was probably in his sixties; he had a grayish gold, neatly kept beard and a mop of gold hair. He was thin—too thin—and had a kind, open face and hazel eyes. He didn't have much with him—just a compact cart covered with blankets and a small, blind dachshund, Loca, who sat on his lap.

Don had had Loca since she could fit in his hand. She was four and a half years old when I met her and had milky eyes. Dachshunds may be small—the biggest tend to be around 30 pounds—but they have huge personalities. Among Loca's quirks: she peed with her leg up, as if she were a male; she tried to climb trees, as if she were a cat; and she *loved* to run through brushy areas, hunting for rats. That's how, Don thought, she'd ended up losing her sight. He suspected her eyes were scratched by bramble when she was hunting one night.

She was crazy all right, which is how she got her name—which Don shortened to "Lo." He pointed to his cart. "This is my whole life. This and Lo."

The moment he was done explaining Loca's habits, Don looked me in the eye and said, "This is not me. I don't want to be here."

"What happened?" I asked. "How did you end up living here?"

"I've been on the street about a year and a half," Don said, "since I got cancer." He'd had an uncle die of colon cancer, and suspected that's what he had when "stuff started to get rough in the stomach." The doctor indeed diagnosed him with colon cancer—there were two cancerous areas, he said, seven inches apart.

Before his diagnosis, Don explained, "I had a home. I had a boat. I had a car. I had a twenty-five-foot cabin cruiser on the Jersey Shore." Don used to spend his days building houses, but as his health was compromised and his medical bills piled up, he couldn't work and had to sell off his assets one at a time.

Don's story is not an unusual one—not even close. A quarter of people in one study said medical debt led to housing problems. And of sixty individuals experiencing homelessness in Seattle, about one third believed their medical debt played a role. The problem just became compounded, as that study showed that if someone had trouble paying medical bills when they were already living on the streets, the length of their homelessness increased by anywhere between two and eleven years.

Don didn't like being homeless, but it didn't worry him as much as Loca's blindness did. He felt the loss of her eyesight as if it had happened to him. "She means sanity. She keeps me here." I didn't press on what "here" meant, but I had a pretty good idea. Don went on, "I always had a dog. A companion. That's the only thing I want, is her eyes done." He looked at me and said he would gladly keep his cancer if his dog could see again.

Recounting that moment gets me every time. The way he was valuing her quality of life more than his actual life. The way I'd felt when Kamon was born and the team of doctors rushed in, and I stood helpless in the corner, able to do nothing but watch. The way I felt helpless when Trinity took him away.

It sucked, too, because in the end, there wasn't much I could do for Loca. I got her in to see a colleague who was a canine ophthalmologist, and after a series of tests she concluded that Loca had glaucoma. Glaucoma happens when something goes awry with the input and output of ocular fluid. If too much fluid builds up in the eye, the pressure then destroys the cells, and the damage is irreversible. We gave Don some medication to ensure Loca wasn't in pain, but she would not ever be able to see.

It was a crappy feeling, not being able to help. I wanted to leave Don with more than just meds for Loca. I assured him that her quality of life was still excellent, because of her incredible sense of smell. I always say that if a dog is going to lose one of its senses, it's much better for it to be vision than smell. Their smell is like their superpower. I did the math once on a dog's sense of smell and figured out that if we had vision akin to a dog's sense of smell, we would be able to be in a plane 30,000 feet up, looking down at a city, and able to read a newspaper on a park bench. That's how impressive a dog's sense of smell is. In other words, Loca still had a pretty great view of the world, even if she couldn't see it.

Don looked reassured but still deeply sad. He never asked for anything for himself, but I wanted to leave him with *something*. I didn't have much in my wallet, but I gave him what I had, and the guys working the camera that day emptied their wallets, too. Don thanked us and walked away. But he came back twenty minutes later, when we were still packing up all of our stuff, with a huge pizza to share.

"Man, what are you doing?" I asked. "You just used all the money we gave you. You didn't have to do this."

Don shrugged and said, "You've been working hard. You look hungry."

* * *

Time after time, I've seen the generosity of people who give away the little they have—to their animals and to other people. I've seen people who you would expect would be completely beaten down by the circumstances of their life, but they approach each day with optimism and are always ready to make a difference in the lives of animals. Perhaps it's because they see in animals what they don't see in all humans: unconditional love.

Richard Lyons, a memorable seventy-two-year-old man I met when I was working in a clinic in Modesto, is one of the greatest animal lovers I have ever encountered. Richard isn't homeless—he lives in a trailer with his wife, four dogs, and two cats. He has gray hair, a long, gray beard, and is thin and tall—he looks a little like a Santa Claus that has been stretched like taffy. He met his wife, Anita, twenty-some years ago when they joined a group for hedgehog owners. Yep, hedgehog owners. Richard's hedgehog was called Munchkin, and he was fascinated by what he called "the little critter." Hedgehogs are really shy and famous for balling themselves up, but they can also be quite social when they feel safe, and can really bond with their owners. They have quills, like porcupines, which seems to make them an odd choice of pet . . . but unlike porcupines, at least they don't shoot them at you.

Richard and Munchkin were living in Tallahassee at the time, and Anita was in San Jose, but through the wonders of long-distance calling a romance born of hedgehog love began. Things got so serious that Richard decided to pick up and move to California. "Me and my Munchkin got on a Greyhound . . . it took five days to get from Tallahassee to San Jose, but I've been in California ever since."

When their hedgehogs died, Richard and Anita weren't sure they wanted to stay in the hedgehog game. Hedgehogs live only four to seven years, and the short lifespan was upsetting to the couple. So it felt natural to expand their family by adopting dogs instead. Their first rescue was Angel, a chihuahua-terrier mix. Then they rescued Poppy. Through these adoptions, Richard came onto the radar of a rescue coordinator from the Humane Society. She called him one night and said, "There's a dog at the pound that's been adopted and returned twice." It wasn't a good predicament—there was a rule at that pound that once an animal had failed to be homed twice, it didn't get a third chance. The dog was going to be euthanized.

"I said, 'I'll be right there.'" That's how Richard met Courtney, a corgi-hound mix. He felt a bond with her instantly. "I said, 'C'mon girl, we're going home.' And I opened the cage door and she followed me out." He can't understand why Courtney didn't work out at her previous homes, because he's never seen her bark in anger at anyone—she's loyal and easygoing. Once Richard was at the park with her when a pit bull came and took Courtney by the neck. "Courtney was whimpering, not even defending herself. The pit bull owners knew there was something amiss with their dog because they gave me fake names and fake phone numbers. I don't blame the pit bull. Pitties are beautiful dogs. Their owners? Not so much sometimes."

Courtney's injuries weren't too severe, luckily, and after a quick vet trip she was as good as new. Then Richard and Anita were out walking their three dogs one night and a little chihuahua came up to them, made a circle around them, then ran off. Then she ran back to them. This process kept repeating. "I got on my haunches and said, 'Come on, little one, either stay or go.' And the next thing I know I've got her in my arms, while I'm still holding the leash for Courtney and Angel." After taking the pup to the vet and having her scanned for a chip, Richard learned, to his disgust, that her owner had thrown her out. The vet said, "Do you want the dog?" And that's how their dog family came to be.

Richard has battled his share of health issues. He served in the military, in Vietnam, and suffers from PTSD. "A lot of people don't understand PTSD," he said. "You read about someone who has done something really horrific, a vet who has gone off the rails. There's a lot of misunderstanding. We're hurting. There's no outward symptoms. I spent thirty-some odd days at the Palo Alto VA, no sharps, no shoelaces, no belt. And if you keep up with what's happening, approximately twenty vets a *day* commit suicide." The stat sounded high to me, so as soon as I got in front of a computer, I looked it up. Richard, sadly, was right.

His dogs, he said, are his life preservers. "Have you ever had a crappy day and then your dog crawls up into your lap and settles down and says 'It's you and me, Pappa, to hell with the rest of the world?'" Though Richard's dogs are not trained service dogs, Richard understood instinctually what studies are now showing: that veterans with PTSD who have a service dog have lessened symptoms and fewer suicidal ideations. The research is compelling enough that the VA is rolling out a program to train service dogs for this purpose.

Having seen firsthand as a soldier the worst of what humankind can do, Richard marvels at the compassion and grace dogs have for us. "I don't know how many hundreds of thousands of years it's been since that first wolf came up to the fire and said, 'Hey, can I lay by the fire for a while?' But since that time, dogs haven't broken that bond. Man has. We break it routinely. We abuse the dogs. Dogs don't abuse us. I have seen cases where they will still lick the hand of the human that's beating them."

Then there are the cats. One of Richard and Anita's cats came to them after they fostered a litter of kittens (they've fostered some two hundred kittens through the years) and couldn't manage giving them all up, so kept one. That's Scruffy. "I'd be very much afraid if Scruffy developed opposable thumbs," Richard said. "She is the most intelligent cat I've ever had in my life." As for Dotty, one night it was pouring rain, and Anita said she could hear a kitten cry.

"No, you can't," Richard said. The sound of rain on their mobile home roof was too heavy to hear anything.

"I can hear it," Anita retorted, and went out in the rain. She came in a half an hour later, a kitten in her arms, and said, "I told you." And that was how Dotty joined the family.

I didn't learn any of this about Richard when I first met him. But I sensed he was a kind man, with a softspoken manner and a slight southern accent. He came in to the clinic because he was worried about Courtney—the corgie-hound mix. She had started stopping to pee at every yard they passed, sometimes peeing twenty or thirty times on the walk down to the park. Richard and Anita had pee pads around the trailer, and he noticed a discoloration on the pee pad. So he brought Courtney in to see me.

I took an X-ray of Courtney's bladder, which confirmed my suspicion that she had bladder stones. I'd seen them in dogs before, but nothing like what I saw in Courtney. She had more than I'd ever seen in any patient, and more than I'd even ever *heard* of—even from back when I was in school and read about crazy cases. Courtney would have felt a constant urgency to go, like there was a weight in her bladder that could never be put down. We'd have to do full bladder surgery.

When I showed Richard the X-ray, he looked stricken, seeing how bad it was, how many stones she had, and, obviously, how uncomfortable it must have been for her.

But when I gave him an estimate of what the surgery might cost—upward of $3,000—he looked resolved. "Well, Doc," he said, "there's no question. Do what you've got to do. Period. I don't care. Courtney's a member of the family. I ain't rich now but I've been poor and I can and will be poor again if that's what it takes."

"Are you sure?" I asked quietly.

Richard nodded. "That's just something that when you become a responsible pet owner, that's what you've got to do."

I asked Richard if I could look into some alternative funding for him, and he agreed, but he wasn't counting on anything.

He talked it over with Anita. "I said we've got to see where we can cut back. There's not a lot of disposable income but there is some—and we can cut out everything except the have-tos. Rent has to be paid. Electric has to be paid, but we don't have to have cable, we don't have to have a cell phone."

I put some information about Richard and Courtney on a Go-FundMe page that I'd started for cases like it. And while I expected to get some donations to help them out, I was surprised by how many came in—all in all, we raised $17,000 in just a single week. In one of my favorite details of all time, Barbara—mom of the cockatoos Boo Boo and Jericho—was one of the donors.

Courtney's surgery went well, we got all the bladder stones out, and when I went out to update Richard and Anita on her condition, I also told them about the donation. Richard was startled, like he was about to fall off his seat. He was shocked. "I'm not a cynic, but you don't see this kind of kindness often. These people don't know me." Richard started to cry.

The money that was left over from Courtney's treatment went into a fund for the other animals' medical needs. And Richard continues to give back himself. "There's a number of homeless in and around my local Starbucks," Richard said, "and a fair number of them have their dog with them. I have seen individuals out there without a pot to piss in. Every possession they own is either in their wagon or shopping cart and they've got their dog beside them. The owners will reach into their sack and give something to their dog. Their dog is the only living thing in their life that accepts them without pushing for anything in return.

I never carry a bunch of money in my wallet, but if I see a guy sitting with his dog and sharing the last of his food with him, then I'll reach in my wallet and share what I've got with him."

Richard and Don are both a bit like me—more adept with four-legged creatures than two-legged ones. They both struck me as exceptionally good men. And I knew that if I sat them down one day and told them all I'd done—how I'd driven drunk, broken a guy's jaw, assaulted a cop who was just trying to help me, and cheated on my wife—they'd say, "You know what, Kwane? It's okay. You're okay. None of us are perfect, we're just doing what we can. And the truth is, we can all be better men."

Chapter 10

THE HUMAN TOUCH

For two years after Kamon's mom and I split up, I lived a rootless life. I moved from San Diego to San Jose to be closer to Kamon, living in a house with three other hapless guys who I didn't know in order to save money. I hit rock bottom when I asked one of the guys for relationship advice one night and he said, "Women are some unstable creatures." He went on with his enlightening lecture as I began to tune out. "They need things the average man can't give them. I just tell 'em, 'Hey, look, baby, what you see is what you get.'" As he wound down his lecture, he turned to say, "All right, boss, need my Zs. Got things to see and people to do tomorrow." Mr. Hallmark himself was in my presence. I needed a change. The house cat gave better advice.

I found a better job and living situation in Los Angeles, but I was hundreds of miles away from my boy again. So every other weekend for a year, I drove six hours, found a hotel, and spent forty-eight hours with Kamon before returning to Los Angeles for work on

Monday. Money was still tight, so I was relegated to sleeping in a Motel 6 or the like while Kamon and I spent our days at the park or mall. I loved that kid, but our time together wasn't ideal. Plus, the driving was more exhausting than I could have ever imagined. The horrific stigma LA traffic carries is well-deserved.

I was also alone with my thoughts much too often. My brain ran in an endless loop of questions: *Why hadn't I worked harder at my relationship? How much would my son be affected by my decisions? What was I going to do with the rest of my life?*

Another change presented itself when, after attending an avian veterinary conference in Monterey, California, I decided to drive back to LA along the coast. Despite my many years in the state, I had never before sought out the famous, landmark Pacific Coast Highway. It was the most beautiful stretch of country I had ever seen. I was so inspired that upon my return home I immediately called the Monterey area to see if there were any practices in need of an associate vet. I found a small neighboring town called Carmel-by-the-Sea. They had been looking for a second doctor for some time. The move would allow me to be closer to Kamon. I knew that being near my son was the only way to answer some of those questions that had been swirling around my head. I needed to feel connected to something bigger than me.

On my first day, I noted that the staff was friendly but stiff. It became clear this was a response to and reflection of the owner, Dr. Bishop, who was strict and impersonal. He made my transition difficult, but after working in five different hospitals in three years, I was becoming used to new surroundings. I was fortunate to have my own private office and I would often retreat there. I suppose the staff sensed my troubles, because it was rare that anyone would voluntarily talk to me.

I was new to the practice, so my client load was very light. On average I would see just seven or eight patients a day, a far cry from the twenty I'd gotten used to. I passed the hours by reading or playing chess online, but it still left too much uninterrupted time for me to ruminate—during work hours and afterward. I quickly learned that Carmel-by-the-Sea was home to a mostly older population, and there wasn't much to do or anyone to do it with. I spent my days mainly by myself, and my evenings in front of takeout and old episodes of *Seinfeld*. My father used to say if there is ever a worry, your mind will find it. How right he was.

So when the receptionist entered my office with my first afternoon appointment on a very slow Tuesday, I leaped up eagerly and greeted an elderly man of significant stature. Standing six-three myself, he was just tall enough to surpass me. He had a large frame and a Santa Claus–size potbelly. He extended a gentle hand and in a deep, smooth voice said, "Hello, I'm Travis Hoover and this is my friend Sammy."

I quickly held out my hand and introduced myself as Kwane (it was a habit I developed early in my career by request of my first employer. He insisted I introduce myself by my first name to men and "Dr. Stewart" to women. He said it was "social professionalism," whatever that means. It seemed like sexism to me, and I introduce myself the same to men and women).

I locked on Mr. Hoover's gaze for a short moment and noticed soft, weathered eyes. He had a warm, childlike smile that rose higher on one side of his face. His thinning, silvery hair was slicked back, and he wore what looked like his Sunday best: slacks, suspenders, and a button-down shirt.

I kneeled down to greet his panting sidekick. Sammy, an overweight border collie, dipped his head, then pointed his nose to the ceiling in a scooping action. I'd come to recognize it as a dog's way to say, "Hey! Come on and feel free to pet me." Border collies are considered to be the most intelligent breed, and Sammy certainly displayed the mannerisms and obedience of a sharp mind.

As I lifted Sammy onto the examination table, Mr. Hoover explained it had been more than a year since Sammy had received a checkup and vaccinations. He grimaced and gently patted me on the back, saying, "My buddy and I need to be sure to get to our doctors on time. I wanna do everything I can to get a few more good years together. I'm approaching the eighteenth green, but just like Sammy I still have a little tread on the ol' tires." He talked very slowly and softly, and would occasionally stutter. I found his presence calming.

While I began Sammy's physical exam, Mr. Hoover took a seat in the chair adjacent to the table. He crossed his legs, leaned back, and asked if I'd ever been to Oregon, his home state. "That's beautiful country, doctor," he stated proudly.

"It's not so shabby here, Mr. Hoover."

I could tell he was eager for conversation, so we talked like two old friends. I learned he was eighty-four, and he told me about his home and tomato garden, then switched gears and spoke about his months in the service during World War II. I opened up about the events that led me to Carmel and the funk that had consumed me. It was rare for me to share personal information with clients. Mr. Hoover now had more intimate knowledge of my life than my own coworkers and even some of my friends.

Sammy was still seated on the exam table staring anxiously at his master, seemingly confused about why he'd been on the stainless steel for so long. My technician cracked the door and said my next exam was waiting. I glanced at my watch and realized forty-five minutes had passed in what felt like ten.

I was sad to see the two go. It had been months since I'd had a meaningful conversation with anyone. Like a goodbye with my late grandfather, I felt like hugging him rather than shaking his hand. He walked out and said he enjoyed talking with me. He didn't have any family or friends around, he explained, and thanked me for treating him so kindly. I saw my own loneliness reflected in him.

As he left I noticed a young lady, about twenty-five, waiting for him in the lobby. She took Mr. Hoover by the arm and escorted him toward the front door. As he exited, he turned in my direction and gave a sincere nod.

By the next day, I'd decided I'd spent long enough feeling sorry for myself. If I wanted to make friends in my new life, I needed to make an effort. I pulled out Mr. Hoover's file and called him.

"Hello, Mr. Hoover, it's Dr. Kwane Stewart from the veterinary office. How are you?"

There was a long pause. "Dr. Stewart . . . Dr. Stewart," he repeated quietly, almost inquisitively. "I'm doing very well today. How are you, sir?"

I told him that I really enjoyed our time together and asked if I could come over on occasion to visit and take Sammy for a walk. The major concern that had come out of Sammy's exam was that the dog was overweight, but Mr. Hoover wasn't able to take him on walks because he wasn't sturdy enough on his feet. I figured Mr. Hoover and I could have some nice chats together, and that Sam could get some exercise afterward. He sounded thrilled and said I was welcome anytime. He simply asked that I call a few days in advance so he could be sure it didn't conflict with his schedule.

I knocked on his door a few days later, and a smiling Mr. Hoover greeted me. "Eleven o'clock sharp," I said. "Right on time. How are you today?"

"I'm well. Give me one second, please." He closed the screen and walked to the corner of the kitchen, then returned with a calendar in hand. He took a minute to read while standing behind the door. "Yes, you are. Come on in."

I had never been to a client's home, and it felt odd at first. He had an old, large four-bedroom house on the corner in a beautiful neighborhood. His home had character but was in dire need of a decorator's touch. Antiques and paintings were scattered throughout the house with little design. The kitchen had appliances that were more than twenty years old. I noticed empty tea boxes and TV dinners stuffed in an overflowing trash can.

He invited me to have a seat on the couch in the living room while he sat a few feet from me next to a dying fire in his reclining chair. The seat of his chair was nearly worn through and had clearly seen many years of use. Sammy jumped up on the couch next to me and laid his head in my lap. He was an affectionate dog and I could tell he remembered our first encounter. Dogs are amazing that way—they not only have an instinct about what's safe and what's not, but they can sniff and identify somebody, usually from a great distance. I'd once been across a huge pasture from Belle and out of her sight. She didn't even know I was there. But when the wind blew and picked up my scent, I could see her nose hit the sky and she started fishtailing her butt in excitement.

Mr. Hoover reached for his remote control, turned down the volume, then immediately jumped into a story about his years traveling the country after leaving the service. It was almost as if he never left the office, as he'd picked up right where he left off. I talked very little as I watched this animated man recount old tales. Every story he told was from decades past. He didn't mention anything that had happened recently, and I suspected it might have been a painful recent past. Perhaps he'd lost his wife.

I glanced at my watch and noticed nearly two hours had passed in a blink. I stood up and looked at Sammy. "All right, buddy, it's your turn." I noticed the leash sitting by the front door. I latched it to his collar and guided him off the couch.

"Where are the two of you going?" Mr. Hoover asked with a confused look.

"I'm going to take Sammy for a walk now."

"Oh, you are? Great! I haven't been able to walk him since I had my stroke years ago and he just loves walks. It's just too dangerous for me with my cane and the streets don't have sidewalks."

"Yes, I remember," I said. "You told me the other day. That's why I'm here." I figured his memory wasn't a hundred percent—he was eighty-four, after all—but it surprised me he couldn't recall the main reason for my visit.

The walk was pleasant and Sammy was perfect on a leash. We returned about thirty minutes later and Mr. Hoover warmly greeted us at the front door. I resumed my position on the couch with Sammy by my side.

"Mr. Hoover, who was the young lady that brought you to the clinic?"

"Drove me to the clinic . . ." I heard him repeat to himself quietly. "That must have been my service."

"Service?"

"Well, I'm unable to drive because I had a stroke some years ago, so when I need to go to the store and run errands, they come and pick me up."

"How often do you actually make it out of the house?"

"Oh, not very often, maybe once a week."

"What about visitors?" I asked.

"The only visitors I have are from the service, I think."

"And me," I said, and smiled. "I have an idea. Why don't we go to lunch next time I come by to walk Sammy?"

His face lit up. "Yes! Yes! That would be super. Will you come by soon?"

His excitement and anticipation gave me a glow, too. "On my next day off, four days from now."

He grabbed his cane and slowly came to his feet. He walked over and grabbed the calendar from the coffee table and asked if I would write down the details of our lunch date. The calendar was littered with appointments, mostly doctors, it appeared.

I wrote in the square for the following Tuesday: "Lunch with Kwane. Walk Sammy."

As I gathered my things and walked out the door, he waved, thanked me, and said he would be counting down the days. As would I.

The weekend passed quickly and I found myself eagerly looking forward to Tuesday. We had lunch as planned in the center of Carmel—the cleanest town I'd ever been to. This place was otherworldy—most of the buildings ran together with a wooden or old brick facade. Dozens of little shops lined the streets, and you'd find a simple floral boutique next to a clothing store that sold $15,000 handbags.

We sat at a table outside a corner deli shop and ate hot roast beef sandwiches. It was a beautiful, rare day when the ocean fog lifted to reveal the sun. Mr. Hoover ate slowly and between bites would look around and smile or nod, acknowledging people passing by, almost as if he were on a parade float. It made me smile . . . and I found myself joining in.

When we arrived back at the house, I hooked Sammy to his leash and took him for a long walk. He was, simply, a perfect dog. I love it when dogs pay attention to you while you walk them, continually looking up at you. It's like they're smiling with gratitude.

Upon our return, Mr. Hoover invited me into the backyard and we walked through his garden. As we sat under a large tree on an old bench, I opened up and spoke about my son, now almost two years old, and shared the details of my divorce. I admitted to Mr. Hoover that I hadn't been faithful to my wife, which had doomed our marriage. Talking about it was difficult at first, but the more I talked, the easier it became and the better I felt.

Mr. Hoover sat and listened, occasionally leaning back and making a soft moaning sound that told me he could commiserate.

"Can I ask you something?" he said at one point, after I'd rambled for ages.

"Of course."

"Why did you cheat?"

I paused for a moment. It's embarrassing to be asked that question. "I was careless and selfish, I suppose."

"No. *Why* did you do it?"

Normally when you give a contrite, remorseful response like I had, people shake their heads and move on. But he wanted to know the "excuse" answer that most people usually throw out first. He wanted to know more about me.

"Honestly, I was a little bored and a woman showed me a lot of attention. And I caved."

"And why was that?"

I don't know if he had training in couples' therapy, but Mr. Hoover helped me wrestle with the loss of my marriage in a way that left me feeling depleted, yes, but also cleansed. I had not said Trinity's name more times in a year than I did that afternoon.

Our Tuesday afternoons together became a routine. For the next month I would walk Sammy and we would have lunch at the deli. I also helped out with some light housework, such as going through his old shed, rearranging boxes, and sweeping the floor.

Each time before leaving him for the day, I would write down our next date in his calendar.

If you define a best friend as someone who knows very intimate details of your life and understands you like few others, then Mr. Hoover had become an unsuspecting best friend. Like him, I was alone in Carmel. He and Sammy had become my crutch and comfort zone—family members and friends in one. I think he felt the same way.

While I was preparing to leave my office one Monday afternoon, a call came in for me. A man with a raspy voice introduced himself as Mr. Dave Jackson, power of attorney for Mr. Hoover. He went on to say that he heard I had visited Mr. Hoover at his home, and he was concerned. He explained that it was his responsibility to monitor Mr. Hoover's encounters with people of whom he was not familiar.

I sat patiently listening to everything he had to say, then explained how I knew Mr. Hoover and how we spent our time together. It did little to dissuade him from his reason for calling, which started to become painfully clear.

"I am politely asking you to end your contact with Mr. Hoover outside of the professional services you provide. And I thank you in advance for your cooperation."

"Mr. Jackson," I said, "may I ask why the stiff monitoring and protection? This doesn't make sense."

"The reasons are medical and they are not something I will disclose. Good day."

The conversation ended abruptly and I felt a rush of anger and disappointment. Why would a lonely, elderly man be deprived of visitors?

The next day I decided I didn't care what Mr. Jackson had to say. His intentions seemed pretentious; so my intention was to ignore him. I knew Mr. Hoover would be hurt if I didn't show up—he was expecting me.

I arrived at Mr. Hoover's as usual and knocked on the door. I was greeted by the same smiling face I had come to appreciate. I noticed he was holding his calendar.

"Did you remember our appointment?" I asked.

"Oh, of course I did." He stepped aside and allowed me to enter.

"I thought I would start by walking Sammy, then we can go to lunch. What do you think?"

"That sounds wonderful. Can I get you some tea first?"

"No, thank you. Maybe I'll have some with lunch."

"Yes, that sounds good. I think I'll wait, too."

As I hooked Sammy to his leash Mr. Hoover followed me to the door.

"I'll wait right here for you guys." He wore a dull, striped brown tie and short-sleeved blue shirt. A worn, tattered wool blazer was draped over his right arm. As we walked away he repeated eagerly, "I'll be waiting."

Over lunch outside the deli, Mr. Hoover smiled even more than usual. As people walked by he would make friendly comments about what they were wearing or try to guess what they were doing for the day. Our time together was so simple.

An elderly lady, close to his age, walked by the table where we were seated. "Hey . . ." I said as I tapped him on the leg. "She's cute." Our relationship had grown very comfortable and he liked my humor.

"She's a little young for me," he chuckled.

I liked his, too.

After lunch I took him by the arm and we took a short walk on the brick sidewalk, occasionally stopping to look into the shops. We sat under a tree on an old bench and had ice cream. While feeling like the day could not have been any better, I started to get a strange feeling, like all these pieces of a puzzle were in front of me, but I wasn't seeing what kind of image they might make.

When we returned to his house, he made hot tea. I began to get comfortable in my usual spot on the couch with Sammy by my side when I heard Mr. Hoover call for me from the other room—not using my name, which he never did, but just saying, "Could you come here a minute?" I followed his voice to a part of the house I hadn't visited. He was going through old photographs.

"This is my mother," he said. It was the first time I had seen him look so sad.

"I miss her." He quickly wiped his eyes, probably hoping I wouldn't see. "I never got married. I never had kids. She was my only family."

We sat on the floor and flipped through dozens of pictures while we drank our tea. His smile returned but his lip quivered as he talked.

"Let me ask you something," I paused. "Do you enjoy having me here?"

"Of course I do. I had a wonderful day." He turned to me and his smile flattened. "Did you not want to come?"

"No, no. I love coming by. I would come by every day if I could." He seemed relieved. "It's just that Mr. Jackson . . ." I stopped myself in mid-sentence.

"Mr. who . . . ?"

"Nothing," I replied. "It's nothing. Why don't we go into the living room and I'll make a fire?"

I made the fire and we took our normal positions. He placed a blanket over his legs and reclined in his chair while letting out a sigh. "Oh, the fire is nice. Thank you."

We sat quietly for about five minutes, then he said, "So tell me . . . what do you do for a living?"

I responded with a soft snort from my nose and a curious smile. Mr. Hoover looked back into the fire, rocking gently in his chair. He had to be joking.

"I'm sorry. What did you say, Mr. Hoover?"

"Oh . . ." He looked back in my direction. "I just wanted to know what you did for work?"

I realized he was serious.

"I'm a . . . a . . ." I had trouble finishing the sentence. "I'm a veterinarian." My eyebrows arched and my voice cracked. "I'm your vet. I take care of Sammy."

"You're a vet." His voice rose with excitement. "That's a wonderful job. You must really enjoy what you do." He sat up in his chair. "Does your family live here?"

It was a sobering moment. Everything suddenly made more sense.

"I think I need to take Sammy to the vet soon," he continued before I could answer. "He's probably due for some shots."

The reason he never called me by my name, the calendar, Mr. Jackson . . . it all became clear.

I moved to the edge of the couch and leaned forward. I clasped my hands together and stared at the floor, then said, "He doesn't need vaccines. I gave them a month ago."

I turned and stared at the fire. My eyes watered.

I shifted to my left and leaned over to Sammy. I gave him a warm hug while I rubbed his long coat. He seemed to crack a smile as I did while we stared at each other. I think Sammy knew what I was thinking. It would be the last time I would ever see them.

I would respect the wishes of Mr. Jackson. I now felt the same way. I wouldn't want a stranger taking advantage of Mr. Hoover. I did not know Mr. Hoover's diagnosis or the extent of his disease. A part of me didn't want to know.

It was hard to think it would be many days before an indifferent visitor from "the service" would come by. It was harder to accept that if Mr. Hoover passed away tonight, the only two creatures that would take notice were sitting right next to each other on the couch.

I stood up and walked to the edge of his recliner and laid my hand on his wrist. "I enjoyed our time together . . . today." I kneeled next to him and slightly tightened my grip. I felt a lump in my throat. "You take care."

He reached across the chair with his opposite hand and grabbed mine. "Can we go to lunch again, soon?"

I looked away for a moment then turned and smiled. "Of course we can."

As I stood up, I pulled the blanket over his legs and tucked it in tight. "I'll write our next date in your calendar on my way out."

"Thank you." He swiveled his chair in my direction as I walked away. "Good night."

When I was out of sight, I leaned against the kitchen wall and took a breath. "Good night, Mr. Hoover." I grabbed the calendar from the counter and wrote: "If you or Sammy ever need anything, anything at all, call Dr. Stewart."

It probably wouldn't please Mr. Jackson, but I taped my business card to the top of the calendar. I peeked around the corner before walking out.

Mr. Hoover had turned back to the fire. He was reclined deep in the chair with his hands interlaced and resting on his chest. He was staring at the fire with a soft grin. Sammy was curled up by his side. I think of that image of them all the time, still today.

My friendship with Mr. Hoover was brief, but it was profound. I was lonely, and sad, and felt I was just floating around in the world.

Having Mr. Hoover for that short period grounded me. It helped me work through the loss of my marriage. It reminded me that my connection to animals wasn't enough, that I might not have a great track record with people, but I needed them. And if they were people who loved animals, well, all the better.

* * *

"There's a guy over there. His dog is sick, I think." The man pointed a finger to the other end of the abandoned lot, where two cars looked to be permanently parked and used as homes.

"Over in the corner there?" I asked.

The man nodded, and Genesis and I made our way across the cracked asphalt. Bald dirt patches sprouted dry weeds; we chose our route carefully over broken glass, smashed cans, and remnants of campsites that had long since been abandoned.

We'd been driving through West Hollywood on our way to visit a Tiny Homes community, and because we had some time to kill instead of running late like usual, we'd stopped at the vacant lot with its smattering of campers and tents. It was a warm August day, and a chemical stench filled the air. I wouldn't have been surprised to learn someone was cooking meth nearby. We approached a few people who looked at us suspiciously, and before they could get *too* suspicious, I said, "Hey, I'm a veterinarian. I'm just going around, talking to people to see if any pets are in need of help." That's how I was directed to Jose and Smiley.

Jose was a thin, small man, and like so many others on the streets, his age was all but impossible to discern because he'd spent so much time out in the elements. I'm not sure I've ever encountered someone more relieved to see me. Usually it takes people a minute or two to size me up and decide whether to trust me or not, but as soon as Jose heard there was a veterinarian on the premises, he came right up to me. Jose was becoming frantic because his chihuahua mix, Smiley, had been in labor for more than twenty-four hours. Even a layperson can tell when a dog is in labor—she was straining, lying on her side, and clearly pushing. Smiley didn't seem to be progressing and was getting tired. Jose was worried about Smiley becoming dehydrated, and he was worried about the health of the puppies.

I carefully examined Smiley where she lay on blankets in a cardboard box, and it was clear to me that she needed a cesarian section to remove the babies. It's a problem I've seen frequently with chihuahuas. They are naturally pretty small dogs, and depending on who they breed with, the puppies can get stuck in the birth canal. Imagine, say, a beagle breeding with a chihuahua. An average beagle is around twenty pounds, whereas your average chihuahua is around four pounds. You don't need to be a scientist to grasp that the physics just don't work out.

It was also clear that the cesarian needed to happen as soon as possible, or else toxins would overwhelm Smiley's system. A cascade of events can send a dog who has been laboring for too long crashing— their electrolyte status changes, they become dehydrated, their blood pressure fluctuates, and their heart rate can, too. Once one body system begins to fail, it leads to others failing. It's like a chair that loses one of its four legs, and collapses.

I was living in San Diego, but still worked off and on with Beverly Oaks Animal Hospital, and I called them to see if I could use their facility to do the surgery. They'd also need staff available to help out with Smiley's recovery. While I waited for a call back from their operations manager and Genesis tended to Smiley, I talked with a tense Jose.

Smiley wasn't his dog, strictly speaking. But he owned her parents, who ran in circles around him, worked up as if they understood what was going on. Smiley was like a grandbaby to him, and he'd given her to a friend named Deanna who lived in the adjacent car. A mixed-breed pup who lived a few cars down was the likely father of Smiley's babies, he explained. Full-term for a dog pregnancy is sixty-four days, and it was about two months ago that Jose had caught the two in the act.

To distract him from the call we were waiting for, and because I was genuinely curious, I kept asking Jose questions about his life, and how he'd ended up on the streets. If I had come up to him as just an interested social worker, I doubt he would have talked to me—he seemed pretty reticent. But we were working together to save an animal he loved; we were together in this. His nervousness also helped drop his guard; he seemed to *want* to talk.

He had been the caregiver for an elderly woman for seven years, he said, making minimum wage—but that was okay, because he lived with her too, so didn't have a lot of expenses. I didn't ask, but presumed that all of his payment was under the table. Then, one day, the woman's son came by and told Jose he had just gotten power of attorney over his mom's assets. He was moving her to an assisted living facility. Jose had three days before he would need to leave.

Jose didn't have much money saved up, and because he hadn't technically been a renter, he didn't have any housing referrals or history to show a prospective landlord. Without any sort of severance from the woman or her son, Jose had very little runway to find a new situation.

He slept in his car for a while, then used what little money he had saved up to buy a trailer, and that became his home. It was lonely, until he found Smiley's parents—strays—and raised them, and then Smiley. He leaned down to stroke Smiley, and as he did, his other two dogs swarmed him, leaping up to get his attention. He tilted his head so they could reach his ears, which both pups promptly began to nibble on.

"My dogs are everything to me," he said. "They keep me going when I don't want to be here. They love me. No matter what else is going on, they are always happy to see me."

He'd had a scare recently, he said. He'd been out doing an errand on his bike, and as he came home and the vacant lot came into view, several trailers—including his—were on fire. "All I could think," he said, "was *Please, God, let the dogs be okay. Take anything—take everything—but not the dogs.*"

A friend of Jose's had been nearby when he saw the flames. He opened the trailer door and, at great risk to himself, had gotten the dogs out. Smiley—who had been terrified—bit him in the process, but the friend didn't let go. All three dogs made it to safety, and Jose gathered them up in his arms as he watched his home burn.

"People drive by and say terrible things to us," he told me. "After the fire, one guy driving by yelled, 'Better ash than trash.'" Jose shuffled his feet. "Us out here, living like this—it's like they don't even see that we're people. But our dogs do."

"I'm really sorry," I said, because I didn't know what else *to* say. I knew without looking at Genesis that this comment would have set her off, that she would be crying. "I can't believe someone would say that to you."

Jose shrugged, and it was that shrug, more than anything he said, that got me most of all. It was like, at this point in his life, he didn't expect anything different from people.

My phone buzzed, and I was relieved to have a callback from Beverly Oaks Animal Hospital. They could accommodate us and reserve the surgery room for me for that afternoon.

"Can you get her there?" I asked Jose. "I have to go to another appointment, but I'll be at the hospital this afternoon to take care of her." I knew that once Smiley got to the hospital, they'd be able to stabilize her, that they could give her an IV and start pumping her with the fluids and electrolytes she needed.

Jose nodded. "My car works fine, Doc. I'll take her."

"And Jose," I said, "when I'm operating on Smiley, it would be a good time for me to spay her so she can't have more puppies. I recommend it. Chihuahas can often have trouble during the laboring process, and given what I'm seeing of Smiley right now, it would not be a good idea for her to become pregnant again."

Jose nodded. "Yes, Doc. Do it. Just save these puppies if you can."

Later that afternoon, Genesis and I made it to the hospital, where Smiley waited for us. I scrubbed in and began the procedure. Once Smiley was under anesthesia, I moved quickly, as the anesthesia can affect the puppies. I made a midline incision and did something we call "exteriorizing the uterus," which just meant pulling the uterus out so I could see what I was working with, if the uterus was still viable, and how many puppies the momma was carrying. There were

three, and so I made another incision and started "milking" the puppies out. The act is a lot like squeezing a sausage out of a casing—
that's even how it was described to us during vet school. I handed
the puppies off to Genesis, one at a time. It was her job to remove the
placenta and start to revitalize them.

They were very still, covered in a white film, and the size of little
mice. Genesis took over their care while I worked on their mom.
Genesis wrapped the puppies in warm towels and rubbed them vigor-
ously, trying to stimulate them. Anytime a mammal is born, rubbing
it helps activate the respiratory center and gets the blood flowing. But
Genesis didn't have any luck. With the help of other available techs,
she rubbed and rubbed, but with no result. The puppies had died in
utero.

I had much more luck with Smiley. I completed the spaying
process, which involved removing her ovaries and her uterus, and
stitching her back up. She'd been through a lot, poor pup, but was
resting and I knew she would heal well. She would be better than
ever, actually, because she wouldn't be at risk of another pregnancy.

I didn't look forward to calling Jose and telling him the news
about the puppies, though. He saw himself as the grandparent, and
had clearly been really hopeful. He had also been through so much
in his life and hadn't had a lot of cause to trust people. Would he
believe me when I gave him the bad news? Or would he think I'd
taken the puppies to sell in order to make a buck, or that I'd given
them to some animal rights organization? He didn't really know me.
Leaving his family in my hands was an act of desperation, sure, but
also one of trust.

I dialed the number Jose had given me and spoke to both him and Deanna. "Smiley's doing great," I told them. "She's resting now. She's going to bounce back from the surgery just fine, and you can come pick her up tonight—just make sure she gets lots of rest."

"Thank you, Doc," Jose said. "Thank you, thank you."

"What about the puppies?" Deanna asked anxiously.

"I'm really sorry," I said—a refrain every veterinarian has said thousands of times. "We tried, but we couldn't save them."

"Oh."

The line was quiet for a long moment, and I heard Deanna sniffle. Then Jose came back on.

"God works in mysterious ways," he said. "He sent you today, didn't He? And look all you did to help me."

I wasn't sure I thought that a higher power had put me in Jose's path. But the circumstances of our meeting were remarkable. Genesis and I had stopped at the vacant lot only because, miracle of miracles, we were running ahead of time, not ten to fifteen minutes late, as was my usual. And while I often came upon animals in need of care, it was rare to come across an emergency situation like Smiley's. If I hadn't happened to stop, Jose might have taken her into the vet. But he wouldn't have been able to pay the fee. And knowing that, he would have delayed the trip as long as possible. By then, as he couldn't be expected to know the medical risks involved in Smiley laboring too long, it would have been too late.

I took Genesis back to her car, then headed home myself. I was glad for the time alone, for some silence.

Genesis was distraught about the puppies, which, knowing her as well as I did, didn't surprise me. She always took it hard when we lost an animal. Despite the fact that she did everything she could, I knew she'd spend the evening questioning her every decision.

I felt more at peace with the day. We had unquestionably saved Smiley's life. We had earned Jose and Deanna's trust. And when Jose had so recently been dehumanized by the "better ash than trash" comment, by coming to his aid, we had reminded him that he wasn't alone, that his love for his dog had worth, and that *he* had worth.

I remembered so vividly a time twenty-five years earlier when someone came to my aid, too—and it wasn't someone I would have expected. I was studying for finals in vet school but couldn't concentrate because I was so hungry. I took a break to pick up some groceries and could practically taste the spaghetti I planned to make. But when I ran my bank card at the checkout, it was declined. I'd run out of money and hadn't even realized it. I was starving, embarrassed because I was holding up the line, and overwhelmed because I didn't know how I was going to make it through the night—let alone finals— without some groceries. I was also angry, probably because I was so damn hungry.

"What do you want to do?" the clerk said, eyeing the growing line behind me.

"I . . . I'm sorry," I finally said, my face hot. "I'm not going to be able to pay for these. Could you put them back?"

"Wait, stop," said the man in line behind me. He was a huge, burly biker guy, his arms covered by tattoos and his face by a beard. "I'll cover it." As he spoke I detected a southern accent.

"Are you sure?" I asked, surprised.

"Yep, I have you." He gave the clerk his credit card, and that was that.

I took my groceries and waited for him outside, to thank him again. "If you give me your contact information," I said, "I can pay you back."

"No need. Just pay it forward."

Until you're on the receiving end of an act of unexpected kindness, it's hard to grasp just how impactful one can be. It's been twenty-five years and I still remember that moment at the grocery store as clearly as if it happened yesterday. I don't remember what I ended up making when I got home—probably the spaghetti—but I remember how hungry I was, and how awful it felt when I didn't think I had access to food, even though I was in the middle of a supermarket full of it. The people I meet like Jose are surrounded by so much wealth, so many resources like food and housing, but it's like they're in a box, cut off from access to it. I remember, too, how I felt *seen* by the biker that day, and how I felt hopeful about the world and the people in it, when just a moment before I'd felt just the opposite. I saved the receipt from that transaction—$64.32—for years. I used it to remind me that people can actually be pretty great.

I always notice bumper stickers that make jokes about how animals are better than humans. The not-so-subtle takeaway is that animals are loyal and kind, while people, basically, just suck. I'm as serious an animal lover as one can be, and yet jokes like these have always bothered me some. I believe that people need animals, yes, but I also believe that people need meaningful connections with other people. There is just no replacement for them. But here's the thing: animals are magical at bringing people together.

Chapter 11

THE ANIMAL LANGUAGE

One day I was talking to my friend Charlie Sammut, an animal enthusiast who ended up starting a zoo. He said the place was built thanks to one of his first exotic animals, a lion named Josef. Josef was so exceptionally calm and sweet that he was recruited to be an animal actor. Josef was, in a word, majestic. And he'd helped build a remarkable zoo. Charlie has elephants, bears, zebras, and panthers, all which take a great deal of money and skill to care for as well as he does. But the animal Charlie was most excited to introduce me to was his chicken. The chicken had had multiple surgeries, and Charlie had spent thousands upon thousands on his care. We don't think twice about spending that kind of money on a lion or an elephant. But a chicken? Charlie took a lot of teasing for his devotion.

"He's a cool chicken," Charlie said, shrugging. "And you know what? It didn't choose to be a chicken."

* * *

My life's trajectory, if you look at it from afar, looks pretty random. From Brownsville to Albuquerque to Colorado, from Milwaukee to San Diego to Carmel, from Modesto to Los Angeles to San Diego once more, my route looks like a jumbled series of stops and starts. But I think it's much more intentional than that. Everywhere I go, everything I do, I collect data that informs my choices. Going back to the university learning center, it could be my pattern recognition, intuition, or my inner fortune-teller. Who cares what it's called? In the end, my choices have done me right.

My choices led me to Travis Hoover, and Travis Hoover led me, ultimately, back to Modesto to be with my son. My choices led me to stop at the 7-Eleven and ask if I could help Kyle's dog with his flea allergy dermatitis. My choices led me to stop and check on Jorge in that abandoned lot in Hollywood. And my choices led me to the actual studios of Hollywood, too.

You've probably noticed what a dog does when it's released into a backyard. Usually, it sniffs out the perimeter, determining if any other animals or unwanted visitors have breached the fence line in its absence. If it sees something amiss—a branch that wasn't there before, for example—it will pounce. Its body is taut, its senses alert. It's like it has extrasensitive sensors and is scanning the premises for safety. Once it has determined that yes, it's safe, it's time to play.

Strange as it is to compare myself to a dog, this is pretty much what I do when I go onto a movie set. It's my job to take in the full scene and make sure the animal actors are safe. It's a job that actually begins much earlier, when I receive a script. I flag the scenes that involve animal actors, and based on the action in each scene, I'll write a risk assessment for that scene and for the movie as a whole. A dog running into a house to snuggle with a little kid gets a low ranking; a horse carrying a rider in the heat, while a dog runs alongside, gets a fairly high one. I'll let the directors and production staff know what parameters and contingencies they should have in place. Then I show up on the set itself to watch the filming.

On set, I'm looking for a wide range of behaviors and, often, I'm looking at a wide range of animals—different species, different ages, different working conditions. I watch to make sure the animals aren't getting too tired, or that their bodies aren't working too hard, that they're not in danger from any other animals being used on set. I watch for signals that they're anxious, or any telltale signs that they might be in pain. My role is to note their every little behavior and interpret it for those who might not catch it otherwise. Then it's my job to tell the director if the animal needs a break.

In this role, I'm also an interpreter of people and their behavior. I work a lot with the trainers—the people who have spent hours and hours preparing the animals for whatever task they're going to be performing that day. The trainers love it when I'm on set, because while they of course know better than anyone when their animals are getting tired, they would rather someone else have the role of telling the director. After all, they want to be hired by that director again, don't they?

I've worked with some incredibly understanding directors and others who have looked at me sideways when I've said things like,

"We need to stop filming so that horse can rest." They're not accustomed to a nobody coming on set and telling them what they can and cannot do, and yet it's literally my job to translate an animal's behavior so that everyone can proceed safely. That's why the "No Animals Were Harmed" certification is such a great tool. If they want the certification, they need to abide by my advice, and animals are protected in the process.

Coordinating movie safety is no longer my full-time gig, but I still get to play the role for Netflix productions, and got to be on set for *The Power of the Dog*. I was by the director Jane Campion's side one day, fascinated by watching her work. I had no idea that *The Power of the Dog*—which stars Benedict Cumberbatch—would be as huge as it was, or that Jane Campion would win an Academy Award for it. I couldn't appreciate everything she was doing, or seeing through her camera lens, and in one sense it was a bit tedious, a lot of hurry-up-and-wait. But as I watched a scene with dozens of cattle, and Benedict Cumberbatch moving through the herd like he was parting the Red Sea, it took my breath away. Not because it was cinematically beautiful, though it was. But because I had this feeling of having come full circle. My love for animals and determination to work with them had come from watching *The Black Stallion*, after all.

My favorite scene in *The Black Stallion* had been at the end, where the Black and his boy, Alec, compete in a challenge match against two of the country's fastest horses and their jockeys. The character Alec was just a little older than I was at the time, and I was mesmerized by his intense, almost primal connection with the Black, with whom he'd been through so much. First he'd saved the Black from a sinking ship, then the horse and the boy survived together on a deserted island, before their eventual rescue and return to the United States.

In the final climactic scene, one of the Black's legs is injured by a competing horse just before the start of the race. Alec, seeing the blood, pulls back. But as if the Black doesn't want to disappoint his boy, he races, pushing through the injury and passing the other horses. The scene cuts back and forth from the action on the track, to footage of the Black and Alec riding on the beaches of the deserted island as they formed their bond. Cheesy? Yes, of course—it was 1979, after all. But it was also beautiful, a cinematic affirmation of the bond humans and animals are capable of. As a boy, I wanted that bond. As a man, it still drove me.

* * *

I'm often asked how I can *read* an animal. And while some of it I can explain, a lot of it I can't. It's like someone can tell you how to get somewhere, but not really what streets to turn on. It becomes just a general sixth sense. It's also taken me *years* of owning, training, treating, and working with animals to develop it. And several bites, too, by the way: eight dogs, two cats (those are the worst because cats carry so much *Pasteurella multocida*, a nasty bacterium that's part of their natural flora), and one python.

The python's name was Pearl. I'd purchased her as a companion for my first python, Percy. Percy, who I got my junior year of undergrad, was a great snake—nine feet long and really docile. I didn't go so far as to let him out of his terrarium when my Doberman Baron was around, but I probably could have—that's how chill he was.

(I'm looking like a better and better roommate, I'll bet.) I thought Percy could do with some company, so I got Pearl—an albino Burmese python. Pearl, a mere six feet long, was not so chill. I put my hand in the terrarium one day, and while I was always on guard that she might strike me, mistaking the warmth of my skin for food, she full-on latched on to my forearm like I was prey, coiled her body around me, and started to squeeze. She was six feet of pure muscle, and while she had her teeth dug into my arm, I was more concerned that she would snap my forearm with her body strength.

That I had misread Pearl's aggressive temperament was my oversight. But you also don't own a python unless you know how to manage them, and so I grabbed the tip of Pearl's tail with my free hand, and began uncoiling her, which snakes have no strength to resist. Then I squeezed her neck to get her teeth to release my arm. The bite wasn't too bad—not nearly as bad as a cat bite—but I knew that Pearl had to go. I sold her to a snake enthusiast, and Percy seemed to do okay on his own after that. And realistically, a crazy Doberman and a nine-foot-long python was probably enough if I ever wanted to have a roommate or a girlfriend again.

Regarding my other bites, I feel pretty lucky to have had only ten in a twenty-five-year career. And I thank my vet techs, who know the cardinal rule, "Don't let the doctor get bitten," and have done a great job holding the animals, or even putting their own limbs at risk. On the occasions where a nervous dog *has* bitten me, the vast majority of them have been German shepherds. It's strange, because as well as I read animals and particularly dogs, I've always had a hard time with German shepherds. They don't give me the cues that other breeds do. Now that I'm wary of them, I think they can probably smell that on me, and so we're doomed together before we even really begin.

Reading animal behavior enters a whole other category when you're dealing with animal actors. Are they tired, or are they just *acting* tired? To figure it out, I watch to see how they recover between takes. Are they bringing less intensity with each cut? Are they shaking? If it's a horse, has it stopped paying attention?

Of all the animals I've observed, it's the dogs that seem the most into it. Which makes sense—they are the pleasers of the animal world. And they like to have a purpose, to be busy. When I was on the set of *Once Upon a Time in Hollywood*, I watched the same scene dozens of times wherein the character played by Brad Pitt owns a vicious pit bull, and sics it on some thieves. The dog was incredibly sweet and affectionate, a teddy bear in a muscled frame. Then, when Quentin Tarantino was ready to shoot, the dog was called to his mark. At the command "Action!" this animal turned into something out of your worst nightmare. He was growling, drooling, baring his teeth, up inside the "thief's" crotch, and acting like he was chewing it out. He was Stephen King's Cujo, fully realized. Then Tarantino called "Cut!" and the dog calmly walked back over to where I stood with his trainer, wagging his tail and looking for some love and treats. He hadn't been trained to be aggressive, he'd been trained to *mimic* aggression. To this dog, it was no different from being told, "Roll over." I've seen scenes like this play out a hundred times, and it always amazes me. When Quentin called animals and actors to their marks again, the dog went right back to work, and the process repeated itself. He was able to do maybe a dozen takes, and though I watched him for signs of fatigue, he was as energetic and scary on the last take as he'd been on the first.

There was a lot of downtime between takes, and at one point, Brad Pitt took a spot to watch the action right next to me. He'd go back on camera when called, then take his place next to me again. We gave each other the "bro nod," like we were two bulls coming into each other's space. I tried not to look at him straight on, but kept kind of peering at him out of the corner of my eye.

A little bit later, I overheard him bragging to an assistant about his own dog. It was something to the effect of how sweet his dog was, how loyal, and how the dog always knew what was going on, that everyone loved him. If I closed my eyes, I could have been on Skid Row, listening to someone on the streets talking about what their dog meant to them.

We wrapped filming early, and I decided to stop by Skid Row and do a little street vet work. Talk about cultural whiplash. The world of beautiful movie stars, five-star trailers, and million-dollar camera equipment was replaced by shoddy tents, abandoned cars and bicycles, and the pervasive scent of urine.

A guy called Dutch greeted me right away. He wasn't homeless but spent his time in the middle of Skid Row, and each time he came to say hello to me. It was my brother, Ian, who told me the score. "Kwane," he said, "you know that guy is the drug runner for this block, right?" After he pointed it out, I noticed that Dutches were everywhere. The streets are pretty organized that way, and territory is claimed by these drug managers in the same way territory is claimed by a cat.

The first time we'd met, Dutch came up to me, very cordial and personable. He wore a clean pressed white shirt, baggy jeans, new sneakers, and chains around his neck. "Hey," he said that first day, "what's goin on, how you doing?" I said hello and explained who I was, and that I was there to help animals. I could see his wheels turning, and he continued asking me questions. "Do you work for anyone? Is this an effort by the city and the police?" I explained that no, I was just an individual, and that I was there to help and if he knew of anyone with a pet who needed veterinary care, it would be great if he could let me know.

After he left, I talked with a homeless guy nearby. "Who is that?" I asked, nodding in the direction Dutch had taken.

"Oh, he just keeps things tight around here. He just makes sure we're safe, we're good."

"Huh," I said, still in the dark. "So if I want to set my tent up next to yours, I gotta go through him?"

"Yeah, kinda. He's kind of looking out for everybody."

"In what other ways is he looking out for you?" I pressed.

The guy just shrugged. He wasn't going to tell me anything. "You know, just lookin' out."

When Dutch greeted me this time, he was particularly talkative. "Dr. Kwane!" he said. "How's it goin', man?"

"How are you, Dutch?"

"I'm good, you know. Just takin' care of my people, donating some money and food. You know, Dr. Kwane, you and me are the same. We're out here helping the people. Anytime you arrive, you need something, you just check in with me. In fact, let me sing you a little song about it."

At this point I couldn't help but grin. "A song? You're a singer, too, Dutch?"

"Oh yeah," he said. "I used to have a good singing career. You know that I know John Legend? Did I ever tell you that?"

"I didn't know that."

"Yeah, and I'm writing songs all the time." He then broke into one he'd apparently written on the spot. "Helping the peeeeeoppple. Ohhhhhh, yeah, Dr. Kwane's out here helping the peeeeeopple."

When he finished, he said, "Aright, man, I'm here. I got you, will make sure you're taken care of, make sure you're not hassled. Anytime you park that car, you just remember to look for me, you ask for Dutch."

Of course, I knew by then he wasn't trying to help me, he was making sure I wasn't trying to push in on his business. It gave me a heavy heart, honestly. If a homeless person went to live in a Tiny Home, they'd be in an environment where they wouldn't be tempted back into drug use. They'd have the incentive of a bed and a shower and food, and if they wanted to stay clean, they had a path to rehab. But on Skid Row, their drug use was a business. On Skid Row, they would feed their addiction until they broke.

After Dutch's serenade, I walked around a bit and it didn't take long before I met a guy named Mateo hanging out outside the public bathrooms with his dog, Fish. Mateo was crazy about Fish, a beagle mix with sweet, floppy ears and somewhat saggy eyes.

"He seems pretty healthy," I said, after checking him out and giving him a vaccine. "Anything you're concerned about?"

"Yes," Mateo said. He wore a large straw hat, spoke quietly, and had the softest eyes I'd ever seen in a human. "We were on the bike the other day—Fish was in the basket. And we got hit by an electric bike and he goes flying off."

"Huh," I said, taking a closer look at Fish. "Did he seem to have trouble after?"

"I thought he was limping a bit."

"Okay, let's have a look. Can you walk him around for me?"

Mateo grabbed Fish's leash and walked in a large circle on the pavement in front of the bathroom, the sound of the cars and surrounding hubbub in competition with the sound of toilets flushing. Fish looked pretty good to my eye, so I asked them to walk a bit faster.

Fish started to prance, and it was like he was showing off a little, for now a few people had gathered, wondering why Mateo was walking his dog in circles like we were at Best in Show and not Skid Row.

"Can you jog with him, just a little bit?" I asked. I was pretty sure he was fine but that would be the real test. Mateo complied, and Fish again seemed to bask in the attention and glory.

"That's a great-looking dog," I said. "I think he should be just fine. Just watch out for those electric bikes."

"He's the greatest," Mateo said. "I can call him from across the whole way and he'll come running to me. He's loyal and true. He always knows what's up. Everyone loves him."

If I closed my eyes, I could be back on set again.

It felt almost surreal. Fish, born in different circumstances, could have been that pit bull on set. He was clearly a smart animal who loved the limelight and loved pleasing his owner. Mateo, born in different circumstances, could have been a movie star. To Fish, Mateo was more than a movie star. He was family.

Chapter 12

LETTING GO

When I went to veterinary school, we had one class—just one—on what to expect when euthanizing an animal. The class was called something like "Changes." We couldn't even call it what it was. The class met one day at a teaching hospital, where we students stood on one side of a glass window while watching a veterinarian at work in a clinic room. No one in the room could see us, though they knew that by bringing their animal to a teaching hospital it was a possibility. We, on the other hand, could see and hear everything.

A professor sat with us and explained we were about to witness the euthanasia process, and that we should pay close attention to the veterinarian's manner and his words. A woman, a man, and two kids stood in the clinic room, but it was set up like a living room, not an exam room. The walls were painted a soft color, carpet lined the floors, and comfortable chairs surrounded a cushy dog bed. The family's chocolate Lab sniffed around the bed.

"Have you ever experienced a euthanasia before?" the veterinarian asked. The man and woman shook their heads no. "Okay," he went on, "here's what's going to happen. First, I'm going to give her a sedative. This will make her sleepy, and relaxed. Then I'm going to place a catheter. She will be very comfortable and can remain right here on this dog bed. You guys are welcome to spend as much time as you want to say goodbye. I'll leave you in here with the door closed. When you're ready for me, you can open the door and I will come back in and give her a solution through the catheter."

The woman and man were clearly trying to hold it together for their kids, but they kept wiping at their eyes. One of the kids—a little girl—clung like Velcro to her mother.

"The solution will stop her heart and her brain activity," the veterinarian went on. "It usually happens within seconds. She will feel no pain. More or less, it's like an overdose of anesthesia, so she will quietly and comfortably drift off, surrounded by her family."

The veterinarian asked for their consent to give the sedation, and soon afterward, the dog looked fast asleep on the bed. "Do you want to stay with him awhile?" the vet asked. His voice was quiet. His eyes were kind as he looked at each member of the family. The mom nodded, and the vet said, "Take your time." Then he left the room to give them privacy.

The whole family cried, and hugged one another, and hugged their dog goodbye. It was an intensely moving, intimate moment in this family's life. I felt almost guilty for watching it. Then they opened the door and the veterinarian came back in to administer the drug that would stop the dog's heart. After three minutes, the vet listened to the dog's heart, then said, "She's gone. Would you like to stay with her?" The mom nodded again, and the family embraced one another, each of them weeping loudly.

In the observation room, we'd been mostly silent. I wiped away some errant tears and noticed others doing the same. One of my classmates, Tyler, started laughing.

Another student, Natalie, turned on him. "What the f— is wrong with you?" she demanded, furious.

"No, Natalie, stop right there," said our professor. "Everybody processes emotion differently. You don't know why Tyler laughed. Maybe he's flooded. Maybe he's feeling something you don't understand. Don't judge him. You'll see people do strange things around death—people act like they don't care, or they'll put on a front so that you can't see what they're feeling, but maybe they'll go home and break down later. You just don't know."

Natalie reddened and looked at the ground. Tyler didn't take the moment to explain himself. I wasn't sure if the professor was right, or if Natalie was right. Tyler was a friend of mine, though, and when we were talking that evening, he said, somewhat out of the blue, "I had a chocolate Lab as a kid. He looked just like that dog today."

And all of it made sense.

Animal euthanasia is hard. It's gut-wrenching to break bad news to pet owners, it's painful to be the primary witness to their grief, and it can be emotionally difficult to carry out. We are taught to be healers, and yet too often—much too often—we must be the ones injecting an animal with a medication that will kill them. Even when euthanasia is done because an animal is suffering, seeing the light leave their eyes because of something you've injected them with, and then listening to make sure their heart has stopped—well, it's a tough role to play.

It is also a role that can be very rewarding. Liberating an animal from their pain is a kindness, and helping an owner come to grips with that and to help them say goodbye . . . it's an honor. My first euthanasia was, mercifully, a very necessary one. I was in vet school, and assisting a doctor one day when a dog that had been hit by a car came in. The injuries to this dog were massive, and there was nothing anyone could have done to save him. When I placed the catheter and put this dog to sleep, I honestly felt that I was helping, that I was ending the severe amount of pain he must have been in.

That was how I framed it when I put my Doberman Solomon down.

That dog . . . I've already said, he was my best, the one I connected with more than any others. But he was terminally ill with bone cancer, or osteosarcoma. He was a young dog—just seven, going on eight—but the outlook for a dog with bone cancer is not good. When I got the diagnosis, I had a decision to make. I could assent to amputating one of his legs, and then subject him to chemotherapy. I didn't like this route at all—not with the survival statistics around osteosarcoma. I didn't want the next year of his life to be recovery from major surgery, then treatment that made him feel ill. Especially not when I knew that the odds of the cancer not having already spread were so slim. And even if he *could* somehow defy the odds and beat the cancer, by the time he was in remission he would be close to the end of his natural life. That wasn't the life I wanted for him. So I chose a course of pain management and monitoring instead, knowing that I would choose euthanasia when pain management no longer worked.

I didn't know it at the time, but cancer in dogs is much more common if dogs were spayed or neutered before they turned one, as Solomon had been.* Now my advice to every owner is not to spay or neuter until the animal is one or one and a half. It's tough, because obviously, the advice I'd given so many owners over the years had been wrong—and the advice I'd taken myself, with my own dogs, had been wrong. It doesn't keep me from trusting science, though. I still trust in numbers, and in data, and I believe that it's a winning strategy in the long term. But there are going to be painful learning lessons, even for science itself.

After several months, it became clear that Solomon was in pain, and that it was time. I wanted to be the one who was with him in the end. It was just the two of us. I gave him strips of steak and took him for a long walk where I let him smell everything he wanted to, even though he was limping along as he did so. Then I brought him to his favorite bed in our living room, where Belle looked on.

Some dogs will lie down on their side in a passive position easily, but that was never Solomon. I could never get him to do that—he hated it. But once I gave him the sedative, he assumed the passive position, and I got down on the floor and lay with him. I spooned him and talked in his ear for a long time. I thanked him for being so solid through my divorce, I thanked him for being so good to Kamon, and

---

* Silvan R. Urfer and Matt Kaeberlein, "Desexing Dogs: A Review of the Current Litera-ture," *Animals* 9, no. 12 (December 2019): 1086.

to Belle. I thanked him for sticking it out in the heat of Modesto and the chill of Carmel when we'd lived there. I thanked him for knowing me so well and loving me so unconditionally.

When I look back at that day, I don't see it as a painful memory but a beautiful one. I see my decision as an act of love for my dog, who asked so little of me and gave so much. If he could have talked, I'm sure he would have said he'd stick around so as not to make anything too hard for me. But it would be for *me*, and not for him. For once, I wanted to do something for him.

* * *

Every pet owner struggles with the same question at some point: How you know when it's time to let them go? I am constantly asked for advice on this issue from clients, friends, and from family. I always tell people to try not to be selfish, to do what will cause the animal the least pain.

At the shelter, of course, it was a different equation, as the animals had no owner to wrestle with the decision. At one point I extended the legal hold time before PTS—or the Put to Sleep order—to ten days, thinking it gave the animals more of a chance to find owners. But that was a huge mistake. Our shelter got overrun with so many dogs, we had an outbreak of kennel cough. The problem was we had only so much money and staff to feed and treat the animals in our care. If the shelter was overcrowded, disease would break out and kill even more animals. It was the worst kind of Catch-22.

Whereas in the shelter I struggled to give the animals just a few extra days, in the world beyond the shelter, my motto is that it's better to put an animal down a month too early than a day too late. Even so, the decision is anything but simple, and sometimes you are just too close to have any perspective. I've sat with countless owners as they've grappled with the decision. I've watched them cry just as I did that day when Tyler laughed. I've learned never, ever to rush these moments—no matter what else is going on in the clinic, how backed up I am, or how much time they need. This is a sacred time between owner and pet, and I want to help them hold it.

In these moments, I'm more like a hospice care worker than anything else. There's no way around the fact that it's a hard time whenever you lose an animal, but I feel a sense of purpose in walking alongside owners as they go through it. And not long ago, I served this role for my mom.

It's no coincidence that it was my mom who took me to see *The Black Stallion*. She loves all animals, but especially horses. She's ridden most of her life, competed in dressage, and cared for Arabians—inarguably the most hotheaded of all horse breeds. I once rode one of her Arabians who decided to get into a race with another horse, despite my pulling up on the reins with all my body weight. This crazy horse took the grudge match at 40 mph all the way into a barbed-wire fence. I bailed at the last minute, but my mom, far from worrying about me, demanded to know why the hell I'd ridden her horse into a fence.

She had Nasamia for twenty-six years, and this horse was her baby. But over the past couple of years, he'd begun to decline from digestive issues he just couldn't shake. Twenty-six isn't ancient for a horse—they live into their thirties—but he was suffering and she didn't know what to do.

I couldn't be there in person for my mom. I'm not a horse vet, and I live halfway across the country. But we talked frequently in the lead-up to her decision to put Nasamia down. It was a strange role for me, because I would go through statistics and medical information with my mom in one tone of voice, the one I reserved for my professional persona. In this voice, I could guide her through the maze of it all as a doctor. But I had another tone of voice that I used—the one of grown son, comforting his mom. It was hard for me to see my mom so sad, and our role reversal felt very acute. I remembered when we'd lost our family dog when I was a boy. My mom had held me and walked me through my grief, whispering, "You gave that animal such a great life. You gave him the best possible care. And I know he loved you for that." On the day my mom put Nasamia down, I talked with her and said exactly the same thing.

I think part of what makes me capable of guiding people through the end of their pet's life is that I don't fear it. It's a natural part of life's cycle, and the constant reminders of it make me less anxious, not more. I didn't want to call euthanizing an animal "Changes"— I thought it was far healthier to call it what it was: "Death." I didn't want Kamon to fear death, either. As we were a family with a lot of pets, he would inevitably witness the death of our pets one day. I thought it might be helpful for him to see how the euthanasia process went with an animal to which he didn't have an attachment. One day when he was about ten and at the shelter with me, a dog came in that had been hit by a car and I had to euthanize it. I explained to Kamon what I was going to do and asked if he wanted to watch. It would have been fine if he'd said no—I knew it was important for him not to feel forced, to only take on what he was ready for. But he wanted to be there, and he was able to be a warm presence for this dog at the end of its life, as I talked him through exactly what I was doing and why.

We had to have an altogether different kind of conversation, it turned out, when we lost Sushi. Ten wonderful years after I brought Sushi home, she escaped from my home on the edge of a canyon. She was always curious about the outside world, but on the rare occasions she got out, she would slink close to the house and then come right back in when something scared her.

Kamon was eighteen, a foot or so taller than the kid he'd been when he begged me to keep the sweet Siamese kitty I'd been a sucker for. He'd spent the years since sleeping with Sushi curled up on his bed each night. He was desperate for us to find her.

We put up flyers, we called shelters, we hoped that her microchip would help someone get her back to us. But after a week, I knew the score. I assumed a coyote had gotten to her, and just hoped she hadn't suffered.

I passed Kamon's room and saw him sitting on his bed, looking defeated. "I'm just so worried about her, Dad," he said. "What if she's cold? Or hungry?" I sat down next to him, shoulder to shoulder, my kid who was just about a man now.

"I'm going to give it to you straight," I said. "I deal with lost pets all the time, and I think we have to assume that she's not going to come back."

Kamon lost it, breaking down like a family member had died. He cried and hugged me, and I cried too. It was our moment of release, our moment to say goodbye. Sushi had been such a big part of my building a new life with my son. It was a hard day but, like the day I put Solomon down, I remember that day with a full heart. Kamon and I shared an intense love for Sushi, and now we were able to share our grief. "We gave her a great life," I told him. "We gave her the best possible care. And she loved us for it."

I would much rather break bad news about a pet to a child, though, than to someone living on the streets. As you've seen on page after page of this book, those who are unhoused rely on their pets more than any of us do. I believe the thought of losing their pet is similar to the idea of losing a spouse; many times people will tear up just talking about the possibility—even if their pet is young, and healthy. The emotion around it doesn't surprise me. It's hard enough for me to lose a pet, with all of the wonderful things in my life. But people who live on the streets have to grapple with questions like "How do I move on without any purpose?" "Who is going to protect me?" "Who is going to love me now?" If they've abused drugs in the past but gotten clean, they have to worry about falling back into those dangerous drug patterns in order to numb the pain. Thinking back to Skye, I'm so glad she got another dog after Lexi died; and Don, Loca's owner, said he, too, always had a dog, that he'd always understood he'd needed one.

I walk the line carefully about advising someone to get another animal. Not because I don't think they *should,* but because everyone processes grief differently. No one can say when someone else is ready. And some don't want to own an animal again, because they don't want to go through the pain of losing it.

Diana, the decades-long volunteer at the shelter, didn't want to risk her heart again after she'd lost the rescues she took in. Charlie, the zookeeper who owned Josef the lion, said he won't ever raise a lion from a cub again. The loss of Josef was just too painful. Charlie was so distraught when Josef died that he went into the hole where they laid the animal and said he would have stayed had his father not reached his hand down and asked him to please come out. Charlie was so distraught he wasn't able to eat or drink and ended up in the hospital with severe dehydration. "There will never be another Josef," he said.

When Genesis brought Pickles home, she cried because she feared losing him. Becoming attached to this dog brought back memories of how hard it had been to lose one. She was terrified. Loving something you know that you will likely outlive is a brave act. Genesis didn't want to miss out on a life with Pickles, so she said yes.

As for me, it took me a while to want another dog after I lost Solomon. But when a job opportunity took me back to Modesto for a short stint, I was very much on the hunt for a Doberman. It felt only right to get one in Modesto.

It was a weird time. Kamon had left home for college, and I was back in the place I'd moved for him, alone. I found a great house and I wandered through it, desperate for a dog to help fill the emptiness.

I went back to the shelter one day to visit my former colleagues and say hi to the new veterinarian, who'd been a classmate of mine at vet school. The shelter had become a great success story, and I was proud to have played a part in it.

I was filled with nostalgia as I wandered through, hit with all the same smells and sounds of so many years before. Then my eyes fell on an adorable puppy—a husky mixed with, of all things, German shepherd. This was *not* the dog for me. I wanted a Doberman. Huskies whined. I had a bad history with German shepherds. I can't explain why I adopted Kora that day, no more than I can explain why my heart melted for Sushi so long before. I knew all too well what the staff did as soon as I walked out of the building. I didn't need to be present to know they smiled at one another and sang, "Sucker!"

Yeah, well, I guess I am.

THE POWER OF ONE

One day when I was working at the Stanislaus County animal shelter, a puppy came in with a badly injured leg from being struck by a car. The puppy was stable but needed a lot of expensive surgery in order to be healthy and adopted out. Given that there was no owner or obvious source of payment, the puppy would most likely be euthanized. For reasons I can't recall, word got out about the case, and a woman contacted the shelter offering to donate $3,000 to save this dog.

Typically, donations to the shelter didn't work that way. We accepted donations, but the money went to a general fund and it was within the staff's discretion how to spend it. Usually we applied funds to whatever would save the greatest number of animals. But the woman was insistent. She did not want to adopt this dog herself, but she did not want him euthanized.

I didn't want to euthanize the dog, either, but I was also frustrated. I went in to vent to the shelter's director. "We could get another vet in here for a day or so and spay and neuter fifty animals for this amount," I complained. "The sooner we can perform the spays and neuters, the sooner these animals can be available for adoption, and the longer they'll have to attract an owner before being placed on the PTS list." The way I saw it, this same $3,000 could save dozens of animals, not just one.

This line of thought might be the only thing I've ever had in common with the billionaire philanthropist Bill Gates. In the documentary *Inside Bill's Brain*, he talks about his decision-making, particularly around the impact of the Bill & Melinda Gates Foundation. "A few years ago," Bill says, "I showed my daughter a polio video because I wanted her to understand, you know, this was this big risky thing we were doing to help lead polio eradication. And the video ends with a girl who's got paralysis limping down the road with the, you know, crummy wood crutch. And so my daughter said to me, 'Well, what did you do?' And I said, 'Well, we're gonna eradicate it.' She says, 'No, what did you do for *her*?'" To a brain like Bill Gates's, the emotional connection is, in his words, "always retail." And to make a dent in disease the way he wanted, "you better think wholesale in, you know, ten-to-the-sixth-, ten-to-the-seventh-type magnitudes." He said he didn't care that that wasn't an inspiring message. "You know," he said, "it's not my goal to be inspiring. The world has limited resources." His goal, he said, was optimization.

That's where I was coming from when I went to the director in dismay.

"I get it, Kwane," the director said. "But we either take this money to save this dog, or we don't. The donor is not offering it otherwise."

I shook my head but left her office. Her hands were tied, too.

So we took the $3,000, we fixed this puppy's leg, and the puppy was adopted almost immediately. All of that, I expected.

What I didn't expect was that it would feel so good to see things through with this puppy. All the techs, all the support staff, and me—we all had become really attached to him. Seeing him bound out of our shelter, happy and healthy, and with a great family, boosted our morale in ways that weren't really quantifiable, but that still mattered. Who knows? Maybe we were all able to stay in the job for just that much longer, or to do it just that much better. What's more, the puppy's story was written up in the press, and spurred more donations than the original $3,000. The implications of saving this dog were porous—we couldn't hold them in our hands—but they were plentiful.

Don't get me wrong—if we are going to fix the many problems of our world, we need to be thinking about optimization. And what I learned that day at the shelter, and what I learn each and every day I go into the streets, is that the singular matters, and the power of one matters. Certainly, I could be a lot more efficient if I bought an RV, outfitted it with all I needed to treat animals, and set up pop-up clinics where people could bring their animals. There *are* clinics like these, and I'm grateful for them. But there is also something that cuts right to the center of my humanity when I go out, on foot, with just a stethoscope, a bag of essentials, and a pouch full of dog treats, and kneel before someone who needs help who might otherwise not have received it.

* * *

I was really fortunate in the course of my street work to cross paths with Jacqueline Norvell, whose work is uncannily similar to mine—as is her philosophy. A little more than ten years ago, Jacqueline—a single mom who works as a legal assistant—was leaving a Lakers game and the taxi went east instead of west. The result was a drive directly through Skid Row, where Jacqueline had never been. It was a Friday night in November, and it was cold. She saw people burning trash to keep warm. She was surprised at how many of the people she saw huddled together were older—elderly, even. There was so much desperation.

She couldn't get the images of Skid Row out of her mind all weekend. When she went to work on Monday, she was still thinking about it. She asked a colleague, "Have you ever been through Skid Row?"

"Sure," the colleague said. "I pass it all the time when I go downtown."

"No," Jacqueline said, "I mean have you been through it?"

The colleague said she hadn't. Something about this ate at Jackie . . . it didn't sit well with her that people were so desperate and that they were ignored and known about at the same time. She announced to her colleague that she was going to do something about it.

"Jaq," the colleague said, "what are you going to do? You're a single working mom."

Jackie thought about it and later called her son, who was away at college. "We're not going to do presents this year," she told him. "Instead, I'm going to use my Christmas bonus to buy food, and we're going to bring meals to people on Skid Row on Christmas."

"What are you *doing*, Jaq?" one of her friends asked when she heard her plans.

"I'm letting the spirit lead me," Jacqueline said.

"Bitch, you don't even go to church!" her friend pushed back teasingly. "Are you dating a born-again Christian or something?"

Jackie's son was supportive of the plan, and while he stayed mostly out of the cooking part, he did wash greens and otherwise helped his mom prepare two turkeys, gravy, mashed potatoes, and a big pot of greens. His dad called and, when he heard the plan, he insisted on going with them to make sure they were okay. Jackie's best friend came, too. The small group scooped the food into to-go containers, loaded up, and caravanned down to Skid Row.

When they got to Skid Row, Jackie let out a whistle to get people's attention. "My whistle is like a sailor's," she said. "And we got bombarded. The food was gone in less than ten minutes."

As she handed out the take-out boxes, people asked her if she had coats, if she had gloves or hats. She didn't have any of that, she said. Just food. But it planted a seed.

Over the course of the next year, she collected coats and jackets from the attorneys in the law office where she worked. "I know you all are going to golf tournaments," she said. "Just bring me the windbreakers you get when you get back." When the lawyers in her office traveled, she asked them to bring her the shampoos, conditioners, and soaps from the hotels. She collected all of it in boxes she placed on a big credenza behind her desk.

The next Christmas, Jackie went back to Skid Row with not only food but also coats, hats, and toiletries. As the years went on, she upped her game, going the first Sunday of every month, and then every single Sunday. Now she has an army of volunteers, and her nonprofit, Brown Bag Lady, has its own space to do meal prep.

Jackie has two gifts I find completely inspiring. One, she listens. When people said they needed coats, she got them coats. As she learned how hard it was for them to keep their hair clean and tidy, she recruited barbers to come out and give haircuts every Sunday. As she learned how many of the people she met had grown up in foster care, she started a camp that brought together foster siblings so they could be reunited for an entire week. She doesn't tell people what *she* thinks they need. She asks the question of them. That in and of itself is an act of great respect.

The second gift Jackie has is the gift of the hustle. She didn't care that people in her law office would turn on their heel when they saw her, thinking, *Oh God, what does Jackie want now?* Sure, she'd ask them to donate. But she saw it as bringing out the best in them. She called up barbers, she called up portable shower services. She felt no guilt in asking. She was convinced she was doing *them* the favor by involving them in her work. In a way, she is like the pastor of yesteryear, when more people actively attended church—she is there to remind people that it's not all just about them. "I just want people to think outside of yourself. It doesn't have to be a big grand gesture. And I don't care who you pray to—you can have a Star of David, you can burn sage, you can wear a cross or rub a Buddha. Just be a good person. That's all it takes, baby."

She also thinks the pandemic helped with that reminder. "The pandemic messed up a lot of people, but it also made so many people stop and take a long, deep look within, and people reached out to me left and right, saying, 'I need to do something in the community.'" Someone who liked to bake cookies started a cookie brigade.

A sixteen-year-old put together individual bags, each holding a shirt, pair of pants, socks, and a jacket, that she carefully labeled with sizes for Jackie to take to Skid Row with her. Whereas Jackie used to have to drive all over and ask people things like "Hey, I see you have an orange tree. Can I have some of your oranges?" Now people seek *her* out and drive across town to bring oranges to *her*.

Once a young lawyer in the office where Jackie works pulled her aside and said, "Jackie, please don't take offense to this"—a tipoff if ever there was one that something bad was coming—"But my husband and I were talking about you this weekend, and it's great that you're doing all of this, but at the end of the day it's a lot and you're just feeding two hundred people a week." The problem of homelessness, the attorney was implying, was much bigger, and Jackie wasn't making a dent.

Jackie had two thoughts, both which she kept to herself. The first was "Yeah, I'm a single mom, an assistant at this office, and I make less than half of what you and your husband do. And I feed two hundred people a week. What are you and your husband doing?"

Her second thought was the same one I've had a hundred times before, which is that you just never know. When you show someone dignity, you don't always see where that goes. A meal isn't always just a meal. A few times, Jackie *has* seen the impact, in that she's had people reach out to her years after she helped them to tell her that she saved their life. All volunteers at Brown Bag Lady are taught to make eye contact. To look every single person in the eye. To call everyone "sir" or "ma'am." To offer to shake hands (before the pandemic). What she wants, when people see her camouflage van drive by, she says, "is for them to exhale." To know that they will be fed, and cared for, and offered dignity.

Jackie now has an army of volunteers working with her. Truth be told, I'm jealous—I want an army, too. But little by little, we're getting there. Street Vet now has backing from Fetch by the Dodo, which means we have more capability to pay for expensive surgeries, treatments, and vaccines. We also have more and more people—some veterinarians, some just animal lovers—who want to volunteer with us, and we're developing the capacity to get them trained.

More than these things, though, I'm most excited by the small, unexpected ways that I see work like mine catching on. I've heard from people in Ukraine who are trying to help homeless pets during the crisis there. I've heard from people who have started collections of flea medications, treats, and food for unsheltered animals. I think I'm most inspired, though, by the way that when people find out about work like Jackie's, or work like Street Vet's, they think, *Huh. Maybe I should get off my couch and do something*, just like I did when I first encountered Kyle and Mutt at the gas station so many years ago. Not everyone can, and I get that. But far more people can get engaged that don't. Far more people can do more than just wring their hands about the problems facing our world than currently do. And maybe I'm just a stubborn optimist, but I think things are changing, and that complacency is losing favor. I think we're all realizing we have *something* to give, something to offer, and that if we all do, maybe we can just change the world.

ACKNOWLEDGMENTS

The journey to become a veterinarian is never done without the support and love of many, as "it takes a village." I would first like to thank: my mother, who passed on her compassion for animals and a love for our natural world; my father, for instilling in me a work ethic and, most of all, integrity (on the day I left home he said, "go chase your dream, but don't leave your integrity behind"); and my brother, Ian, for helping me build this wonderful mission.

Thank you to the folks at Ross Yoon, especially Jenna Free, for helping me build the book, and Tina Pohlman, for being my advocate. Thanks to my editor Sydney Rogers, for her keen eye, and the rest of the HarperOne team, for believing these are stories that need to be shared with the world. I also want to thank the many people who agreed to share their stories for this book. I don't take your trust lightly and hope I have done your stories justice.

Beyond that, there are so many others who have shaped me, inspired me, motivated me, picked me up when I fell, and shown me love when I needed it most. You know who you are. Collectively, it was all of you who are responsible for creating "The Street Vet." And through the Street Vet Project, you have treated, helped, and saved so many four-legged souls and helped restore faith to their owners that there is a lot of good in the world. Kindness is the essence of being human.

ABOUT THE AUTHOR

D r. Kwane Stewart grew up in New Mexico in a pet-loving home and committed to working with animals when he was just seven. After graduating from Colorado State Veterinary School, he worked in nearly every facet of the profession, from leading a shelter to protecting animals on film sets for Netflix. Now he devotes his time to his "true calling," providing free medical care to the pets of our unhoused population. He walks the streets of Los Angeles and San Diego searching for and treating the pets most desperate for care.